LOOK BACK TO THE FUTUR

Consecrated Women in Britain 597 A.D.

Published by DWM Press (Roscommon Ireland) & Debra Maria Flint (2021).
Printed by:
DWM Press
Donamon Castle
Co. Roscommon
Ireland
Co. Roscommon (2021)

Debra Maria Flint was born in Birmingham to a non-Catholic family and converted to Catholicism at the age of 21 years. She lived in Greece from 1975 – 1983 and speaks and writes fluent Greek. Debra studied for an Oxford University Diploma in Theology and Philosophy from 1984 – 1986. While studying in Oxford Debra met Bill Flint and they later married and eventually moved to the South West of England. Debra's husband was a Roman Catholic theologian who wrote several religious books. They had one daughter, Azelina, who is now a university lecturer.

After her marriage Debra trained as a psychiatric nurse and also obtained a BSc in health and a post graduate certificate in legal investigative practice. She worked in healthcare for over 20 years. Debra was also elected as an independent member of a local council.

Debra's husband died in 2014 and she decided to follow a vowed path within the Catholic Church. Debra spent several years exploring the new and restored forms of consecrated life and experienced the difficulties that many women in Britain face when trying to take up one of these paths. She now plans to take private rather than public vows in order to retain her independence and her ability to speak out forcefully on the need to promote the female consecrated life.

Debra is also trained in Ignatian spiritual conversation and bereavement counselling. She currently lives in Scotland and 'Look back to the Future' is her first book.

Dedication

This book is dedicated to the memory of three people who always looked out for me:

Irene Doris Keen
Frederick Keen Senior
Frederick Keen Junior

Acknowledgement

With grateful thanks to my friend Michael Egan SVD. Without his unwavering support and encouragement this book would never have been completed and published.

Contents

Introduction

Chapter One
Anglo Saxon Vowed Women

Chapter Two
Richeldis, the Mysterious Widow

Chapter Three
Virgins, Widows and Mystics

Chapter Four
Pre-Reformation Decline and Post Reformation Exiles

Chapter Five
Active Religious Congregations (Modernists and Reformers)

Chapter Six
Post Vatican II Decline and Beginnings of 21st
                    Century Renewal

Chapter Seven
Female Consecrated Life in Britain Today

Conclusion

Introduction

'Look Back to the Future: Consecrated Women in Britain 597 AD to date' is written as a historical tour of the past in which I look at the ministries and influence which women have held in the Catholic Church in Britain since 597 AD to date. Within this book I clearly demonstrate that, although women in the Catholic Church have never been priests, their influence was once far greater than it is today. For example, the majority of monasteries in Anglo-Saxon England were usually founded by a devout aristocratic woman of high birth who would preside over a community of nuns and would also preside over a parallel but separate community of monks and priests. These monasteries were known as Double Monasteries and the women who presided over them were known as abbesses. Abbesses were not priests since women could not be ordained and so they did not celebrate Mass or administer other sacraments. However, their inability to administer the sacraments in no way affected their prestige and influence. They presided over abbeys of great learning and from their monasteries came a new cultural rising of the people. They also hosted or attended synods of the church. St Hilda was host to the famous Synod of Whitby which sought to determine the date when Easter should be celebrated. The Abbess Aeffled who succeeded St. Hilda also attended a church synod. She attended and spoke at the Synod of Nidd and persuaded King Aidfrith to change his mind and restore St. Wilfrid to the Bishopric.

It would be true to say that the Anglo-Saxon period was probably the one where women were at the height of their influence in the Catholic Church in Britain but within this book, I also demonstrate that there were other women of great influence during other historical periods. These include the mysterious Richeldis who founded the English National Shrine of Walsingham and the mystic, Julian of Norwich, whose book *'Revelations of Divine Love'* was the first book to be written in English by a woman. This book led to her being regarded as one of the greatest Christian mystics of all time. However, during her own times, she was mainly sought out for her spiritual direction. Julian of Norwich was an anchoress who took vows of chastity singly, rather than as part of a group, and her vocation appeared to flower up until the reformation alongside another vocation where women took vows singly - that of the vowess. A vowess was a widow who took vows of chastity singly after the death of her late husband. These women owned property but used their property and what they owned to further the mission of the Church.

The vocations of singly consecrated women such as anchoresses and vowesses flowered prior to the reformation alongside the vocations of women in religious orders who lived in enclosed convents. The reformation, however, led to the destruction of all forms of female consecrated life when King Henry VIII separated the English Church from papal primacy. The religious orders were eliminated as were the anchoresses and vowesses who had generally attached themselves to churches and monasteries. The female consecrated life was completely suppressed in Britain until the early eighteenth century and up until then women who felt a call to be consecrated usually went abroad to Europe to achieve this aim. However, when these women went abroad it was to join convents of enclosed women. The single vowed life which had been annihilated by the reformation did not begin to re-appear again in the Catholic Church until the 1940's when some war widows began to take vows in other European countries.

In the late sixteenth century, following the reformation, Pope Pius V declared solemn vows and strict enclosure to be essential for all consecrated women. This was challenged by the English woman Mary Ward (1585 – 1645) who wished to set up an active religious congregation for women on the lines of the Jesuits. This form of active religious life would seek to educate girls in general in the way that boys were educated. However, all her attempts to do so were suppressed by Pope Urban XIII in 1631 and it was not until the late eighteenth century that a new form of active female consecrated life, based on her idea, began to flourish in the Catholic Church in Britain and Europe. But this new form of active consecrated life required all religious women to live in convents albeit not enclosed. Both the single vowed vocations of anchoress and vowess remained lost. Within the Anglican Church there was also a revival of the female consecrated life which began with the Oxford Movement in the mid nineteenth century. This brought about a revival of the Anglican religious orders but, as with the Catholic Church, the single consecrated life remained lost in this case until the early twenty first century.

The active female religious life flourished in the Catholic Church in Britain in the late eighteenth, nineteenth and early twentieth centuries but began to wane after Vatican II. However, the waning of this form of religious life in the late twentieth century was certainly not due to Vatican II alone. There were a number of other factors which caused this and these included: the Catholic laity taking on more ministries (which was a result of Vatican II); the British government taking over the provision of education and care; a reluctance of the active religious to promote their own vocations after Vatican II perhaps because of a loss of direction; the restoration of the Order of Consecrated Virgins and also the Order of Consecrated Hermits which offered women the opportunity to take vows singly; an unwillingness of some of the male hierarchy to promote the active female religious life and the association of a small number of religious congregations with institutional abuse. All these factors led to a decline in this form of religious life from the late twentieth century onwards. However, the enclosed female religious life, which had also re-appeared in Britain in the centuries after the Reformation, continued to flourish in both the UK and Ireland because this vocation is a very specific form of contemplative life and there will always be some rare women who feel called to an enclosed life of prayer.

Today I would argue that there is much confusion within the Catholic Church in regards to female consecrated life in Britain. The ancient vocations of consecrated virgin and hermit have been restored but are not yet fully understood by the laity. The ancient vocation of consecrated widow (formerly vowess) has been partially restored in that it was approved by Pope St John Paul II in Vita Consecrata and consecrations are now taking place under local rite. However, a final universal rite for this vocation has yet to be approved and enshrined in canon law. Another new form of consecrated life that of member of a secular institute, has also appeared in Britain but has never taken off here in the way it has in Europe probably due to, among other things, a lack of support from the Catholic hierarchy. Meanwhile the active female religious life is experiencing a decline in numbers while, as previously stated, the enclosed religious life continues to hold its own. So, there are many different forms of female consecrated life existing in Britain but there have been very few attempts to describe or promote these in any cohesive manner. All this has led to confusion around the female consecrated life and many Catholic women have not even heard of the new and restored vocations and think of consecration as simply being a 'nun'. However most consecrated women are not nuns at all. Officially, under Catholic Canon Law, only enclosed religious women are nuns and even the active religious do not qualify for this title. Nuns are consecrated women who are both enclosed and who have also taken solemn vows. All other consecrated Catholic women, including those in active religious orders, take simple vows. This confusion about the female consecrated life in Britain has sadly contributed to the fact that here, in the main, only priestly vocations are currently being promoted while female vocations are generally being ignored.

This book has been written with a strong Catholic slant and is particularly aimed at the Catholic community in Britain because it is within that community in particular that women are struggling to find full time vocation and ministry. One of the main purposes of this book is therefore to dispel the current confusion and ignorance in regards to the female consecrated life and to promote the vocations of consecrated women in modern Britain. The other main purpose of this book is to look towards the future for women within the Catholic Church. I raise the question of how the female consecrated life and other ministries could develop within this church in the twenty first century.

I argue that there should be a much more concerted effort in the British Catholic Church to promote the new and restored forms of consecrated life as these enable consecrated women to be fully emerged in the modern world and to act as a leaven. These forms of consecrated life have also never been promoted in Britain in the way that they have in other European countries and very little is known about them here. I believe that if they were better known they would attract more interest as they enable a woman to live independently in the world and to follow a career while also putting God and prayer at the forefront of her life. Basically, they enable contemplation in action.

In conclusion I also argue that if the Catholic Church is serious about increasing the involvement of women in its midst then the logical development would be to allow both consecrated women and lay women to become lay cardinals. This is because although women have never been ordained, they have in the past presided over or attended church synods. The current obsession with the ordination of women within the Catholic Church could be schismatic and it also nurtures the fallacy that the only role of any importance in the church is that of the ordained priest. This fallacy is perhaps what

Pope Francis terms 'clericalism'. There is on occasions a complete obsession with the fact that only the ability to say Mass matters in the Church and, if a person cannot say Mass, their ministry amounts to nothing. This is a fallacy because in the past both abbesses and anchoresses have held ministries that were different from the ministry of a priest but were regarded as equally important. The abbess ruled over double monasteries, taught theology to would be priests and voted at church synods. The anchoress gave spiritual direction to both priests and kings. Active female religious have also in past centuries been trail blazers who have set up hospitals for the poor and promoted the education of girls at a time when it was not socially acceptable for girls to be formally educated. Thus, the earlier church and in particular the pre-reformation church was much more egalitarian and inclusive. It was a community-based church made up of people exercising many ministries and did not revolve around the ministry of one priest.

It would be theoretically possible to create women lay cardinals within the Catholic Church because lay cardinals have previously existed and there is no theological reason why they cannot exist again and why women cannot hold this role. In the past lay cardinals were men who were never ordained as deacons, priests or bishops and did not consecrate the eucharist. It has today become commonplace to think of a cardinal as the next order after bishop to which a man can become ordained. In fact, the position of cardinal is not a position to which one can be ordained and the title of cardinal is an honorific office in the church independent of the priesthood. Therefore, as lay cardinals were not priests there is no reason why they cannot in the future be women. The appointment of women as lay cardinals would restore their influence within the church while paying respect to tradition (in the sense that women have never been priests but have previously voted at church synods). It would therefore connect with the past and would show the modern world that the Catholic Church values the contribution of women today as much as it valued it in the past. 'Look back to the Future' is therefore the title of this book.

Chapter One

Anglo Saxon Consecrated Women

Ah, bride of Christ, bright fame on earth is thine.
More bright in heaven thy bridal torches shine.
Exultant hymns proclaim in glad accord;
No power henceforth may part thee from thy Lord.

St Bede; Ecclesiastical History of the English People

It is not possible to know when Christianity first came to Britain due to the fact that in the first, second and third centuries very little was written down.

An ancient legend states that it was Joseph of Arimathea who first brought Christianity to Britain and that the first Glastonbury Abbey, which has long since been destroyed, was built upon his order apparently to house the Holy Grail. This legend is not as far-fetched as it may seem bearing in mind the trade routes of the time. In fact, if Joseph was a wealthy merchant, it's very possible he could have visited Glastonbury. It is indeed very odd that Joseph of Arimathea should have been linked particularly with Glastonbury if he had not actually visited and what is even odder is another legend; the legend of the Glastonbury Thorn.

This legend states that it was Joseph, himself, who brought the thorn to Glastonbury. This thorn is different to other common hawthorns in England as it flowers twice a year both at Christmas and in the spring. The common English hawthorn flowers only once a year in the spring. This thorn is called Crataegus monogyna var, biflora and it is native to the

Middle East. There have been many attempts in England to grow this thorn from seed and direct cuttings but all these attempts have resulted in a reversion to the normal British hawthorn type which flowers only in the spring. The Glastonbury thorn can only grow in this country by being grafted on to the common hawthorn and as a result of this it grows in Glastonbury only. Some people might state that this could give some credence to the Glastonbury legend.

Due to the fact that literacy in Britain was extremely far from universal in the early centuries we do, to a large extent, depend on legends and will never know exactly when Christianity arrived in Britain. However, the first strong evidence is from the late second century AD. This is confirmed by St Bede, England's first historian. He reports that in 156 AD, during the reign of the Roman Emperor Marcus Antoninus, a British King named Lucius wrote to Pope Eleutherus in Rome requesting instruction in the Christian faith. At this time Roman Britain was very cosmopolitan and merchants from all over the Roman Empire came to Britain. It is therefore highly likely that by this time Christianity had reached Britain and may even have become well-established. However, despite this, Christianity had yet to be approved by the Roman Empire and Christians were persecuted wherever they were.

St Alban was Britain's first Christian Martyr and he was executed in a town called Verulamium in 304 AD. Much later an abbey was built there and dedicated to St Alban and the town became known as St Albans. However, in 312 AD very shortly after St Alban's death the Roman Emperor

Constantine while at the Battle of Milvian Bridge apparently looked up at the sun before the battle. It is recorded by Eusebius of Caesarea that when he did so he saw a cross of light and the Greek words 'Ev Toutw Nika' (pronounced on touto nika) which means 'with that conquer'. Constantine commanded his troops to adorn their shields with the Christian symbol and thereafter they were victorious. As a result of this in 313 AD Constantine granted an edict of tolerance to all religions including Christianity and the persecution of Christians ceased.

In 314 AD, only one year after Constantine's decision to cease the persecution of Christians in his Empire, it is significant that three British bishops attended a church council in Arles in France. These three bishops were Eborius Bishop of York; Restitutus Bishop of London and Adelius Bishop of Caerleon in Gwent. What is significant is that three bishops were produced so quickly to attend a church conference after Constantine granted tolerance to all religions. Clearly Christianity had become very well established in Britain prior to Constantine's edict and that is why these bishops could suddenly be produced to attend a conference. This almost certainly confirms that Christianity had arrived in Britain in either the first or second century and had become quite well-organized in certain areas by the early fourth century. However, at this time Christianity was still far from being universal and in 597 AD St Augustine of Canterbury, who was a Benedictine monk, brought the Benedictine rule to England. This led to a further growth in the Christian faith.

By the late sixth century, when Augustine brought the Benedictine rule to England, monasticism had been flourishing in Europe for some time. In 320 AD St Pachomios, an Egyptian who had converted to Christianity, had established a religious community in Tabbynesis under the authority of the Bishop of Tentyra. This community was male but St Pachomios almost certainly also established the first female religious community. At the time of his death in 346 AD he left two nunneries as well as the nine monasteries for which he is more renowned. His nunneries were probably established around 335 AD. However, there was also a tradition of women, particularly widows, taking single vows in Europe and we are told that a canonical widow took part in the eucharist and prayed with psalms, hymns and meditations. (*Testamentum Domini*, 4th-5th century). Some of these widows such as Paula and Marcella (4th century) eventually established religious communities for women while others remained in their households and gave alms to the poor.

By the sixth century female celibacy within the Christian Church was becoming increasingly prominent and the firm establishment of this vocation at that time was becoming synonymous with monasticism. This was particularly the case in England and Wales where the monastic life was becoming very well established. However, there were also widows who became single vowed women from Anglo Saxon times and they are referred to in the Penitential of Archbishop Theodore of Canterbury (668 -90) and the Confessional of Egbert, Archbishop of York (732-66).

While the Benedictine rule was the first form of monasticism to arrive in Britain, this rule was shortly followed by other rules such as the Celtic rule of St Columba. However, the first English nuns were probably Benedictine.

The formation of community religious life and the establishment of the same was different in England to all other countries with possibly the exception of some parts of France and Germany. This was because in England, while there were some all-male religious communities, there were no all-female religious communities. Female religious became established in double houses. These houses consisted of monks and nuns living in separate dwellings side by side which were almost always led or presided over by a woman. Women abbesses in the Anglo- Saxon Catholic Church enjoyed great power and prestige. In fact, they had far more influence than any woman has in the British Catholic Church today.

Each double monastery in Anglo Saxon England was usually founded by an aristocratic woman of high birth who would rule a community of nuns and a parallel but separate community of monks and priests. These women were known as abbesses. They were not priests since women could not be ordained and so they did not celebrate Mass and administer the sacraments. However, their inability to say Mass in no way affected their prestige and influence. These women presided over abbeys of great learning and from their monasteries there came a cultural rising of the people. The abbesses received the same training and learning as monks. Some of the abbesses also taught and trained future bishops.

For example, five of the men St Hilda taught and trained became bishops and a sixth was elected but died before he was ordained. The abbesses were also sought out for their spiritual counsel and when Aldfrith, King of Northumbria died, he chose two abbesses to whom to convey his last words and instructions. In the later church or in the church in other parts of Europe it would have been the bishop who received such a prestigious call, but in Anglo- Saxon England it was the abbess.

The first phase then, in the history of the female consecrated life in British Catholic Christianity, is a matriarchal one. Here were women who presided not only over their abbeys, but also over society as a whole. Stenton (writing in 1943) describes Christian England as led by all powerful women. But what of the women themselves? Who were they and what exactly did they achieve? Some of these women are examined in more detail below.

Perhaps the most well-known of all the great Anglo-Saxon abbesses is St Hilda and she, like most of these powerful Catholic women, was of royal blood. Hilda was born in 614 AD and was the great niece of King Edwin. At the age of 13, in 627 AD, Hilda was baptised at the court of King Edwin by the Roman missionary Paulinus. After Hilda's baptism virtually nothing is known about her until she reaches 33 years of age. Fell (1981) argues that during this period she was probably married and widowed as the first English historian, Bede, never refers to her as a virgin. She had earlier planned to travel to France and join the monastery at Chelles but this was only shortly before she established her first monastery in

England. While on route to France she was called back by Bishop Aiden who gave her a small plot of land on the Wear where she established her first English monastery. She later became Abbess of the monastery at Hartlepool before eventually founding the Abbey at Whitby (then known as Streoneshalch) in 657 AD. This abbey was regarded as a place of great holiness of which St Bede writes;

'After the example of the primitive church no one was rich, no one was needy and everything was held in common.'

Hilda had become renowned for her great personal charity but this was not the only quality which she possessed. Under her direction the abbey at Whitby became famous for its learning and Hilda taught theology to five men who later became bishops. Hilda was also hostess to the famous Synod of Whitby which was presided over by King Oswy. Mitchell (1995) argues that it is interesting that Oswy chose Whitby to host the synod rather than an all-male monastery. She states that had Hilda not been a very gifted teacher and administrator the location of this synod would be very difficult to explain. This synod was of national importance because it sought to resolve a conflict between two different strands of Christianity (known as the Celtic and the Roman) as to the date Easter should be celebrated. Hilda actually supported the Celtic dating of Easter at the synod although she accepted the Roman dating when this was eventually decided. Hilda's Abbey at Whitby, over time, became used as the burial place for Kings and other royal personages in the north of England and would have had a significance not unlike that of Westminster Abbey today. Hilda was a woman of great personal energy and even though the last six years of her life were spent in illness and suffering, this in no way diminished her drive. She died on the 17 November 680 AD and her cult was soon widespread. Fifteen ancient English churches were dedicated to her.

A contemporary of St Hilda was Queen Etheldreda (otherwise known as Aethelthryth and also a canonised saint). St Etheldreda was born near Newmarket in Suffolk and was one of four daughters of King Anna (or Onna) of East Anglia, all of whom eventually founded abbeys. Etheldreda was first married to Tondberct who was a Prince of South Gyrwas or the Fens. She managed to persuade her husband to respect a vow of virginity which she had made prior to her marriage. However, Tondberct died within a couple of years of the marriage and Etheldreda retired to the Isle of Ely which she had received as a mourning gift. Shortly after this a marriage was arranged for her to King Egfrid. This marriage was arranged for political reasons and was not the will of Etheldreda. Her husband was in his teens and several years younger than she and Bede states that the marriage was never consummated. Initially King Egfrid, probably because he was so much younger then Etheldreda, had agreed not to consummate the marriage but he later changed his mind. However, Etheldreda did not wish to consummate the marriage and pleaded with her husband to allow her to enter a double monastery. He reluctantly agreed and she became a nun at Coldingham while he later re-married. Etheldreda became a woman of great influence and renown. She founded the double monastery at Ely in 673 and from there her fame spread. Etheldreda's influence seems to have been due to her humility rather than her royal lineage as she was renowned for the life of poverty that she led. Etheldreda ate only one meal a day and spent the whole night from matin (around mid-night) until dawn in prayer. This would have impressed the people of her day because she had exchanged wealth and comfort for ascetism. Several years after becoming Abbess of Ely Etheldreda died of a tumour in the neck. When, seventeen years later, her sister decided to remove her body and place it in a new coffin it was found to be incorrupt. This miracle was attributed to Etheldreda's virginity as both virginity and celibacy were regarded as being of great worth in the society of her day. Her body was placed in a stone sarcophagus and her shrine was frequently visited. Sadly, the shrine was destroyed in 1541 at the time of the reformation.

Following Etheldreda's death she was succeeded as abbess by her sister Sexburg who was the widow of King Eorcenberct of Kent. Sexburg was in turn succeeded by her daughter Eormenhild, widow of Wulfhere, who was the first Christian King of Mercia. Mitchell argues that there was a dynastic succession of abbesses in Anglo-Saxon England and there can be little doubt that this was the case. Another example of this is that of the Kentish Princess Domneva who was married to a son of Penda, King of Mercia. This marriage ended so that both partners could found monasteries. Domneva founded Thanet Minster in Kent around 670 AD. Her daughters were: St Mildrith, who succeeded her as Abbess of Thanet; St Mildburg, who was Abbess of Wenlock; and St Mildgyth.

St Mildrith, also known as Mildred, was educated at the prestigious royal Abbey of Chelles and she later entered this Abbey as a nun apparently to avoid the attentions of an unwanted suitor. She was determined not to embrace the married state and after she had successfully avoided her suitor, she returned to the Abbey at Minster in Thanet which her mother had founded. She became abbess and was well known for her generosity to the poor and after her death her tomb became a place of pilgrimage. Her sister, Mildburg, also acquired the position of abbess. She took over the monastery at Wenlock which had been founded by her father. Mildburg became renowned for her miraculous healing powers and after her death her tomb was venerated. However, following the Danish raids in the ninth century, her tomb fell into disuse and was lost. It was rediscovered around 1079 and several miraculous healings were alleged to have occurred. These healings were recorded by Otto, Cardinal of Ostia. This led to five churches being dedicated to her and her feast, which is the 23 February, being celebrated in the English Calendar of Saints. Mildgyth, who was the sister of Mildrith and Mildburg, is also recognised as a saint but very little is known about her other than that miraculous powers were believed to have been exhibited at her tomb in Northumbria.

While many of the famous abbesses of this age presided over double monasteries in their own country there were also Anglo-Saxon women who presided over abbeys overseas. Some of these women were also at the forefront of overseas evangelization and one such woman was St Leoba.

St Leoba was distantly related to St Boniface who was a pioneer of missionary work and the missions he organized extended into the eighth century. He established the first organized Christianity in many parts of Germany. He is the patron saint of Germany and was the first archbishop of Mainz. He is also known as the 'Apostle to the Germans'. Boniface developed a very close relationship with Leoba and he gave her a great deal of authority. Leoba had originally become a nun at Wimborne under the Abbess, Tetta. However, in 748 she was asked by Boniface to aid him in the evangelisation of Germany and this may have been because Boniface believed women would give his mission more credibility. Boniface had established a convent in the town of Bishofsheim and this was where Leoba became abbess. However, she was not only in charge of her own house but also of all the nuns who worked for Boniface. In 754 AD, when Boniface was preparing a missionary trip to Frisia, he gave his monastic cowl to Leoba to indicate that while he was away she was his delegate. This demonstrates that these were days when women were very highly regarded in both the English and European Catholic Church. Leoba was a very learned woman and she was also involved in the foundation of nunneries at Kitzingen and Ochsenfurt. She came to be regarded as wise in counsel and was sought out by magnates of Church and state including bishops in Fulda; Pippin III and Hildegaard, wife of Charlemagne.

In her later years Leoba retired to an estate near Mainz with some other Anglo-Saxon nuns. She died on 28 September 782. St Boniface had requested in his will that Leoba be buried in his own tomb (which would suggest they had a deep spiritual friendship); however, when Leoba died she was placed near to him but not in his grave. Several miracles were attributed to her graveside and she was canonised. Her biography was written by Rudolf of Fulda 50 years after her death and in it she is described as Orthodox in faith; patient in hope and generous in charity. While she became very well known as a saint in Germany, she was little known in the country of her birth or in her native south west. This was presumably because news did not travel fast then and her many achievements were never reported back to her native country and town.

St Leoba was not the only Anglo-Saxon woman who was at the forefront of the Christian evangelization of other countries in Europe. There were others. Another such example was St Tecla of Kinzingen. She is believed to have been born in Southern Britain and she was a relative of St Leoba. Originally Tecla was a nun at Wimborne in Dorset before she, too, was recruited by St Boniface to become a nun under Leoba at Bishchofsheim. Later she became an abbess herself at Ochsenfurt and Kitzingen respectively. Tecla did not achieve such renown as Leoba but she is mentioned in ancient liturgical books as a saint. Her feast day was kept on the 15 of October.

Another woman who travelled overseas and who deserves mention here is St Ercongota. She was the daughter of King Erconbert of Kent and his wife St Sexburga. Ercongota went overseas to join two of her aunts at the Abbey of Faremoutiers-en-Brie near Meaux in France. This Abbey was also a double monastery with communities of monks and nuns over which an abbess presided. Its first abbess had been St Fara. Ercongota did not travel to France to evangelise, as there were already double monasteries in France at this time and France was already Christian. She travelled to France because she felt she had a vocation to be a nun and her aunt, St Sethrida, was Abbess of Faremoutiers-en-Brie at that time. Ercongota died young and so was never an abbess. However, she seemed to achieve particular renown in her time as she was regarded to have been of outstanding virtue and also to possess the gift of prophecy. She was certainly aware of her imminent death and it is recorded that she visited many of the older nuns in her abbey to tell them she was shortly to die. Apparently, on her passing, many of the men who lived in the double monastery where she resided said that they saw a great light and heard the sounds of music. Three days later a balsam like scent was alleged to have wafted from her grave and this was believed to be a sign of her sanctity. St Bede, Britain's first historian, who narrated these events, stated that many other wonderful deeds occurred but he did not have the time to narrate them all.

The women mentioned above are just a few of the many Anglo-Saxon women who either presided as abbesses over double monasteries of men and women in this period or who were significant during this period for other reasons. It has also been noted that the 'Abbess Phenomenon', where-by a woman presided over a great double monastery of men and women, occurred not only in England. It was prevalent in France at the time and the Anglo-Saxon abbesses also took this phenomenon to Germany when they evangelized it. It was a phenomenon that existed in these Western European countries between the early seventh and late ninth centuries. It would be true to state that all the abbesses concerned were of royal or aristocratic birth. However, this is hardly surprising as during this period it was only the well-off or aristocratic of both sexes who received an education. Mitchell states that there was a network of double monasteries with abbesses related to each other, some of them connected by marriage with several English kingdoms and often linked with French monasteries. While this is undoubtedly true it in no way takes away the equality that these women had with men during this period of church history. Yes, these women of influence were highly connected, but so also were the Christian men of influence during this time. The poor did not receive an education. The most important thing to note here is that while within the English Church and the Churches of France and Germany, there had developed a tradition that priests should be male; the inability of women to become priests in no way diminished their importance or their influence. The tradition that priests should be male had developed as a result of the fact that at the last supper only males were recorded to have been present. However, this did not mean that Jesus did not value women. Overall, the Gospels suggest the contrary. Jesus was a liberator of women. This can clearly be seen for example in the Gospel of John where a woman is brought to Jesus having been caught in the act of committing adultery. The scribes and pharisees wished to stone the woman but Jesus stated that only he who had never wronged another (sinned) could throw the first stone and all the scribes and pharisees left one-by-one. After this Jesus simply advised the woman to 'go away and sin no more' (John 8:11). But when he did so he had already dealt with and condemned the men who had bullied her and dared to think that they were better than she was. Jesus valued women and his endorsement of women was clearly reflected in the positions they held in the early Christian Church.

Within the Anglo-Saxon Catholic Church of this time men and women were at least equal. If they were not equal then society was matriarchal and it was women who had the most influence as most or all double monasteries were run by women. At this time men and women appeared to have two very distinctive and separate roles. While men said Mass and administered the sacraments women, it seems, were the administrators and learned intellectuals of the day. They presided over the main centres of learning and also over the education of some men. They had some responsibility for both governance and administration and had a role which is in many ways similar to that of a bishop – apart from the fact that they could not administer sacraments. They attended church synods and clearly expressed their views at these synods. It is known that Hilda hosted the Synod of Whitby and that she supported the Celtic dating of Easter, although she accepted the Roman calculation when she found herself in the minority. The participation of a woman in such a synod is significant today because within the current Catholic Church only male bishops generally vote at synods. The Pope has recently appointed Sr Nathalie Becquart to the position of undersecretary to the Synod of Bishops and given her voting rights but this is just one woman and she does not have the influence that Hilda had. St Hilda was a very important and influential figure who clearly played a part in church politics. It is known that she tried to prevent Wilfrid from regaining the see of Northumbria after his first expulsion in 678 AD by Archbishop Theodore. She wrote to the Pope to express her view on this matter and clearly felt able to do so. This incident shows just how far the profile and influence of Catholic women has fallen over the centuries. Catholic women of today are generally not able to officially express an opinion to a Pope as to who should be a bishop. They also play no part in this selection process.

Hilda was succeeded as Abbess by Aelffled who was also literate, independent and powerful. Stephen of Ripon, a contemporary of Wilfrid who wrote his biography, describes Aeffled as the best adviser in the Kingdom. She was involved in the public lives of kings, abbots and bishops and was sought out for her advice. She too, also attended church synods. Aeffled, unlike Hilda, supported Wilfrid's restoration to the see of Northumbria and she attended the Synod of Nidd in order to express her views. She spoke at the synod and persuaded King Aid-frith to change his mind and restore Wilfrid to the Bishopric. Aeffled, therefore, was one of the most influential persons at this synod.

All of the Anglo-Saxon abbesses of the double monasteries of the early seventh to late ninth century enjoyed an education on a par with the education of men and many of them taught future bishops. Indeed, they were highly regarded as theologians. This again illustrates to us how the influence of women has declined in the British Catholic Church over the centuries. Today the Catholic Church led by Rome has very few female theologians with whom it officially consults. Of course, there are female theologians in Western Europe but sadly many of these are not consulted by the Vatican. However, these past abbesses were highly regarded in England, France and Germany as theologians. They also studied ancient law; rules of allegory (in order to interpret the scriptures which suggests that they probably preached quite often); grammar; spelling; punctuation and metre (for composing verses in Latin). The abbesses were clearly versed in Latin which was the language of the church. We know this because St Leoba sent verses in Latin, which she had composed, to her friend, relative and mentor St Boniface. What is also significant is the fact that a large majority of these women were canonised after their death. In fact, there are far more Anglo-Saxon female saints than there are male. This would again suggest that society at this time was more matriarchal than patriarchal.

Mitchell (1995) cites the main reason for the disappearance of the double monasteries as being disapproval from the Church of Rome. She states that the hostility of Rome was inevitable bearing in mind the church's disapproval of the sexuality of women from Eve onwards. However, it is clear from the actions of the early female saints and from the writings of St Bede that all the Anglo-Saxon abbesses preferred the celibate state and had actively chosen it. These abbesses were not therefore in conflict with Rome. Celibacy was seen as a legitimate choice for a lifestyle in most European cultures during the early Christian centuries and not just in the Roman one. Indeed, the idea that a single or non-sexual life can be fulfilling, continued for many centuries and was accepted in Britain until at least the 1950's. There were many women in relatively modern times (not necessarily Catholic or Christian) who chose not to marry or have a sexual relationship but instead to remain single and dedicate their whole lives to a career such as nursing or teaching. The idea that every woman must have penetrative sex to express her sexuality is a relatively new phenomenon.

The real reason for the disappearance of the double monasteries was almost certainly the Danish raids. Viking raids began in England in the late eighth century and the monasteries were targeted. This was due to the fact that the monasteries were wealthy and had valuable objects which could easily be moved. The first monastery to be raided was Lindisfarne in 793 AD and from then on, the Vikings continued to raid Britain for almost a hundred years. By the late ninth century the Vikings had conquered most of the Anglo-Saxon Kingdoms that made up England at the time. However, Alfred the Great, King of Wessex, did manage to defeat the Vikings at the Battle of Edington in 878 AD. Following this the Danes had control of northern and eastern England while Alfred and his successors controlled Wessex. Eventually the whole of England was unified with Norway and Denmark in the eleventh century during the reign of King Cnut. The Vikings, in the writer's view, had no respect whatsoever for women and their virtual conquest of the whole of England would have left an indelible stamp on the country. The monasteries were looted and destroyed and some Christians were pelted to death. A great many of the shrines dedicated to the Anglo-Saxon matriarchal saints were destroyed at this time and their relics were lost. Women were not generally valued in Viking society and were often used as sex objects in bizarre rituals at Norse funerals. Norse society, which was brought to England at this time, was male dominated and women's responsibilities were clearly defined to the domestic. In the Scandinavian countries a woman was prohibited by law from participating in most political and governmental activities. She could not be a chieftain or a judge and could not be a witness or speak at assemblies. Obviously, this was in complete contrast to the situation in Anglo-Saxon England and one can only imagine the shock and change of status that the Vikings brought to the influential Anglo-Saxon women when they invaded their monasteries. The great abbesses were deposed and with them went their unique and influential role. This was a role that has never again been seen in the British Catholic Church as the women appeared to have many responsibilities that were later only given to bishops, cardinal deacons and lay cardinals.

Chapter Two

Richeldis – the mysterious widow

A noble widow, sometime lady of this town
Called Rychold, in living full virtuous
Desired of Our Lady a petition
Her to honour with some work bounteous

(The Pynson Ballad)

The name or term 'Rychold' or 'Richeldis' refers to a woman who founded a shrine to Our Lady of Walsingham in England at a date that is disputed by historians but which is most likely to have been 1061 A.D. It has been argued (Flint 2014) that the term 'Richeldis' may not actually have been a name at all but a description of a woman which could mean 'rich and fair'. Very little is known about Richeldis and, as we will see further below, her identity is disputed within Christian circles. What is not disputed however is the fact that this lost lady of mystery had some kind of a vision of the Virgin Mary, the results of which had a major impact upon English spirituality until the time of the reformation and continue to have an impact on Christian spirituality within multi-cultural Britain today. The other thing that is not disputed is that Richeldis was certainly a widow. She was also probably a consecrated widow. These widows were known as vowesses and they existed in Britain from Anglo Saxon time's right up until the time of the reformation.

The Order of Consecrated Widows is one of the oldest female forms of religious life in church history since it existed in the early church and is referred to in the New Testament (1 Timothy 5: 3-15). At that time, in order to be enrolled into this Order, a woman had to be at least 60 years of age, to have been married only once and to have lived a life of prayer and service to others following the death of her late husband. During this period there were also Orders of Virgins and Orders of Bishops and Deacons. (Rees 2015). However, the Order of Widows very quickly became well established in the early Church and is mentioned by several of the early Church Fathers such as: St. Polycarp; St Hippolytus and St Jerome (Rees 2015). These widows were mature women of faith who took part in the eucharist; prayed with psalms, hymns and meditations and were also known for their intercessory prayer. There is evidence that the Order of Consecrated Widows existed in Britain from the Anglo-Saxon period right through to the reformation. This is because consecrated widows are mentioned in both the Penitential of Archbishop Theodore of Canterbury (668-90) and the Confessional of Egbert, Archbishop of York (732-66). Egbert's Pontifical includes a blessing of widows and their habit, and a rite for consecrating widows during Mass. There are also other mentions of consecrated widows (vowesses) which are of a later date than the time of Richeldis and are held in diocesan records. Vowesses were answerable to their diocesan bishops and from Anglo Saxon times until the time of the reformation they wore a particular costume. This consisted of a cloak or mantle and a ring. There is no actual evidence that Richeldis was a vowess but it can be argued that it is highly likely that she was one. This is because vowesses tended to be widows of substantial means who used their own money for the further promotion of the

Christian faith and Richeldis was certainly a woman of means who is referred to as the once lady of the manor in the Pynson Ballad. She also used her own money for the further promotion of the Christian faith.

The village of Walsingham is situated in the countryside approximately five miles from the north Norfolk coast. Today Walsingham is a small village with a population of around 850 people. It is still famed for its shrines to the Virgin Mary of which there are currently three and these are Anglican, Catholic and Orthodox. However, the original shrine which was founded in 1061 was destroyed in the sixteenth century. While Walsingham is still famed for its shrines to the Virgin Mary, these current shrines do not have the national importance or significance that the original shrine acquired prior to the reformation. This is due to the fact that Britain is now a secular state. Dickinson (1956) stated that it was very remarkable that the original shrine ever acquired any great importance bearing in mind that it began as nothing and was erected (according to the Pynson Ballad) by the widow of the parish in a small village which was then a backwater and has again become a backwater today. However, Walsingham is only 28 miles from Norwich and Norwich was one of the largest cities in England prior to the Norman Conquest in 1066.

Most of the information we have about the foundation of the Walsingham Shrine and the vision of the lost lady of mystery comes from a ballad which is today called 'The Pynson Ballad'. The author of this ballad was Richard Pynson (1448 – 1529) who was one of the first printers of English books.

Pynson may have been a Glover before he turned to printing. He was recognised for printing law texts and religious books. He began his printing career in 1492 and became printer to Henry VII in 1506. It is not known exactly when Pynson published what is today known as 'The Pynson Ballad' although academics state it was probably sometime during the later reign of King Henry VII. While this ballad is today known as 'The Pynson Ballad' – it was originally known as 'The Foundation of the Chapel of Walsingham'. It is possible that this ballad may have been printed later than is generally postulated (1495). This is because this ballad represents the history of what had become one of the most famous shrines in Europe. During the reign of Henry VIII, it may have begun to seem obvious to the printer that this shrine was under threat and that may very well have been the motivation for the printing of this ballad.

Flint (2014) states that while the ballad was printed in the sixteenth century it was clearly of the early Norman era. He argues that the ballad was passed down through the oral tradition of balladeering. The ballad was the medium by which the good news stories of the day were broadcast. The ballads were sung or proclaimed in castles and halls by a balladeer. Flint's hypothesis is actually confirmed by the ballad itself which states that 'the chronicle' gives witness to four hundred years of history. Chronicles represented accounts of local or distant events over a period of time. They were started by an individual chronicler and carried on for many years by continuators. The ballad states:

'Foure hundredth yere and more to cronacle to witness

Hath endured this notable pylgrymage
Where grace is daily shewyd to man of every age.'

'Four hundred years and more so the chronicle gives witness
Has endured this notable pilgrimage
Where grace is daily shown to man of every age.'
(Translated by Flint 2014)

Flint (2014) also states that the Pynson Ballad celebrated the history of what had become one of the most famous shrines in the whole of Europe. The ballad dates the foundation of the Shrine as 1061 and then goes on to describe how the shrine was founded. It states that a widow who used to live in Walsingham desired to do something for Our Lady and prayed to be honoured with the commission of some bounteous work. Richeldis then apparently had a vision of the house in Nazareth where the Holy Family had once lived and was asked to build in Walsingham an imitation of this home in which the Annunciation of Archangel Gabriel had occurred. Apparently Richeldis had some difficulty in discerning where this holy house should be built and the shrine was eventually built in a different place to where the first foundations were laid. The ballad then states that since its original foundation the shrine has stood for over 400 years and many miracles have occurred on this site. It gives the reason for this as the fact that the shrine is a new Nazareth and England is Our Lady's dowry. It is curious that this ballad, detailing the whole history of the shrine which had up until then been passed down in the oral tradition, should suddenly have been written down and printed just prior to the reformation. One therefore assumes that the reason for this may have been a very definite sense of threat which was felt by those who loved the shrine. Perhaps they expected it to be destroyed and the tradition of balladeering and pilgrimages to cease.

Dickinson (1956) investigates the rise to fame of the Walsingham Shrine since its foundation. He states that the sudden rise of the shrine to fame (after the time of its origin) was very curious. He speculates that this may have been due to the foundation of a Priory of Augustinian Canons there, after the foundation of the shrine, as at this time there was an increasing veneration of monasticism. Other attractions may have been the fact that the shrine was believed to be an exact copy of the Holy House or the lure of the healing wells which adjoined the original chapel of Our Lady of Walsingham. However, according to Dickinson, the most important factor that led to the rise in fame of the shrine of Our Lady of Walsingham was probably the growing devotion to the statue of Our Lady there. Another factor may, of course, have been the personality of the foundress herself which has been lost to posterity. Richeldis was almost certainly a vowess and she may have been a woman of exceptional character. Records of her were probably destroyed during the Norman conquest of 1066 and any remaining records would have been destroyed during the later reformation.

The fame of Walsingham drew many pilgrims from all over the country and from overseas and their route can be traced along a pilgrim way. People from Scotland and the northern counties passed through Lincolnshire, crossed the Wash and assembled at King's Lynn. They then proceeded past the priories of Flitcham, Rudham and Cokesford. Those coming from the east passed Norwich and Attlebridge whilst the route from London led through Newmarket, Brandon and Fakenham. Along these various pilgrim routes there were wayside chapels which were erected at intervals. Today only two of these wayside chapels survive and these are the Chapel of Our Lady of the Red Mount and the Chapel of St Catherine of Alexandria which is at Houghton-in-the-dale about a mile from Walsingham. This chapel is also known as the slipper chapel as at this point pilgrims used to take off their shoes and make the rest of their journey barefoot. Today this chapel has become what is known as the National Shrine of Our Lady (Catholic).

It is believed that the current Anglican Shrine of Our Lady of Walsingham stands on the site of the original chapel to Our Lady of Walsingham which was erected by the widow known as Richeldis. From the first foundation of the original chapel there is a long record of miracle cures and remarkable answers to prayer. One Knight, Sir Ralph Boutetourt, who was been pursued by his enemies in 1314 was reputed to have been saved from death by Our Lady's intercession. The Pynson Ballad also describes the occurrences of many miracles and cures at Walsingham:

'And Syth here Our Lady hath shewyd many myracle,
Innumerable, nowe here for to express
To suche as visyte thys hir habytacle,
Ever lyke newe to them that call her in distress.
Foure hundredth yere and more to cronacle to witness

Hath endured this notable pylgrymage,
Where grace is daily shewyd to man of every age.'

'And ever since Our Lady has shown many miracles here,
Innumerable, too many to be expressed here
To such as visit this her abode,
Ever like new to them that call her in distress.
Four hundred years and more so the chronicle gives witness
Has endured this notable pilgrimage,
Where grace is daily shown to man of every age.
(Translated by Flint 2014)

As a result of the growing fame of the shrine since its original
foundation it was visited by many national dignitaries of royal
blood. Richard Coeur de Lion was the first of these. He was
followed by Henry III who was a frequent visitor and made at
least 11 pilgrimages between 1226 and 1272. This King was
also a generous benefactor of the shrine and bestowed (to
those who managed the shrine at that time) many gifts
including forty oak trees for the work of the church in one
year and two years later another 20 trees. He also gave 40
shillings to the shrine annually and many gifts of wax and
tapers. He paid for a golden crown to be placed on the
original statue of Our Lady of Walsingham. Sadly, this statue
was eventually destroyed during the reformation. However,
prior to this disastrous event the son of Henry III, Edward I,
visited Walsingham on at least 12 occasions staying for
several days at a time. Also, at Candlemas in 1296
Walsingham provided the setting for the signing of an
instrument between King Edward and the Count of Flanders.
This clearly indicates that by this time Walsingham had

become a shrine of great importance. After this time many more royal dignitaries visited the shrine. These included: Edward II in 1315; Isabella Queen Dowager of France in 1332; Edward III in 1361; Queen Johan widow of Henry IV in 1427; Henry VI in 1455 and Edward IV in 1469 and Henry VII (the father of Henry VIII) who made a pilgrimage to the Walsingham Shrine in 1487 and later sent his banner as a votive offering to Our Lady's Shrine after his victory over Lambert Simnel in the battle of Stoke.

The last royal visitor to the Shrine of Our Lady of Walsingham prior to the Reformation was King Henry VIII himself. He visited the shrine in 1511 when he was staying at East Barsham Hall close to Houghton–in-the-Dale. In the early years of his reign, he had a great devotion to Our Lady of Walsingham and his Exchequer Book records many gifts to her shrine. These include a contribution of £20 in 1511 and a contribution of £23 eleven shillings and four pence in 1512. Henry VIII also paid twice a year for a candle to be kept burning at the Shrine of Our Lady of Walsingham and for the wages of a priest to say Mass there. The payments were made regularly until 1538. However on 29 September 1538 an entry was made in his Exchequer Book which stated – 'For the King's candle before Our Lady of Walsingham and to pay the Prior for his salary, nil'.

It is true to say that since the 15th century the English Catholic Church had become in need of reform and that the shrine of Walsingham, along with the rest of the English church was not exempt from this. However, the fact that there were abuses at Walsingham at the time of the reformation does not detract from the remarkable achievement of the widow Richeldis who had founded a shrine in the eleventh century that had brought much spiritual consolation to many people for over four hundred years.

In regards to the Shrine at Walsingham at the time of the reformation, the once small hamlet of Walsingham Parva had grown to be a large town with many shops and inns. There were 17 inns in the then large town of Walsingham and apparently the inn-keepers there were renowned for overcharging. Indeed, shortly after Easter in 1431, there was a great fire in which four of the inns were destroyed. The origins of the fire were never proved but according to recorded rumour the fire had been a revenge for the excessive charges that inn keepers made to pilgrims on their way to Walsingham. It would seem that due to the increasing renown of Walsingham some of those who either run the shrine or were associated with it were becoming corrupt.

The corruption of those who actually run the shrine was confirmed when in 1514 the Bishop of Norwich visited the Walsingham Priory. He found, on the testimony of members of the community there, that the Prior was leading a scandalous life. Apparently, he had taken a concubine and was appropriating for his own use the riches belonging to the shrine. This Prior was actually removed from office and the abuses were remedied prior to the reformation but never-the-less these abuses would have tarnished the reputation of those running the shrine. These abuses also opened the way for King Henry VIII, who by the time of the reformation had become a sexist royal despot, to plunder the monasteries. King Henry VIII was not actually anti-Catholic at all and the irony of the English reformation is the fact that he had previously been given the title of 'Defender of the Faith' (i.e. the Catholic Faith) by Pope Leo X as a result of a pamphlet he wrote entitled *'Assertio septem sacramentorum adversus Martinum' or 'Declaration of the Seven Sacraments against Martin Luther.'* However, King Henry had later become driven by two motives and these were his desire to marry Anne Boleyn and his desire to fill his exchequer with the money from the many monasteries across the country.

Henry VIII appointed Thomas Cromwell to suppress the monasteries and in 1536 Cromwell organised a series of visitations which led to the suppression of smaller foundations. Cromwell was politically motivated and the then Prior of Walsingham, Richard Vowell, was happy to go along with him. However, a substantial number of Augustinian Canons belonging to the community at Walsingham were not in agreement with the prior and one of these included the sub-prior. This sadly led to his death and in 1537, while the prior was apparently 'sucking up' to Thomas Cromwell, the Sub- Prior Nicholas Mileham was charged with conspiring to rebel against the lesser monasteries. He was convicted of high treason and hanged outside the priory walls. Eleven people in all, including the sub-prior, were hanged, drawn and quartered. The following year, in 1538, Prior Vowell agreed to the destruction of the Walsingham Priory and assisted the King's commissioners in the removal of the statue of Our Lady and of many of the gold and silver ornaments. The image of Our Lady was publicly burned at Chelsea along with other famous images which had been held in veneration. As a reward for his compliance Prior Vowell received a pension of £100 a year which at the time was a massive amount of money perhaps the equivalent of £100,000 per year today. The 15 canons who had supported him also received pensions.

The destruction of the Walsingham Priory and Shrine gave rise to an anonymous ballad known as the The Walsingham Lament. This ballad was anonymous for obvious reasons but is believed to have been written by Philip, Earl of Arundel, the eldest son of the Duke of Norfolk. He was the second cousin once removed of Queen Elizabeth I and was committed to the Tower of London in 1585. He was imprisoned there for ten years until he died in 1595. He was canonised by Pope Paul VI in 1970. The ballad is as follows:

In the wracks of Walsingham
Whom should I chuse
But the Queene of Walsingham
To be my guide and muse?

Then, thou Prince of Walsingham
Graunt me to frame
Bitter plaintes to rewe thy wronge
Bitter woe for thy name.

Bitter was it, oh to see
The sely sheepe
Murdered by the raveninge wolves
While the sheepharde did sleep.

Bitter was it, oh to view
The sacred vyne

Whiles the gardiners plaied all close
Rooted up by swine.

Bitter, bitter oh to behoulde
The grasse to grow
Where the walles of Walsingham
So stately did showe.

Such were the worth of Walsingham
While she did stand
Such are the wrackes as now do showe
Of that (so) holy lande.

Levell, levell with the ground
The Towres doe lye
Which with their golden, glitt'ring tops
Pearsed oute to the skye.

Where weare the gates noe gates are nowe,
The waies unknowen,
Where the presse of freares dis passe
While her fame far was blowen.

Oules do scrike where sweetest himnes
Lately wear songe,
Toades and serpents hold their dennes
Where the palmers did throng.

Weep, weep, O Walsingham,
Whose days are nightes,
Blessings turned to blasphemies,
Holy deedes to dispites.

Sinne is where our Ladye sate,

Heaven turned is to helle;
Sathan sitte where out Lord did swaye,
Walsingham, oh farewell.

Following the destruction of the Walsingham Shrine in 1538 there remained no shrine on this site for hundreds of years. And yet.... The vision of the mysterious Richeldis, who was almost certainly a consecrated widow, did not die.

After over 360 years one Charlotte Pearson Boyd purchased the Slipper Chapel in 1896. This chapel had been built in 1340 a mile outside the original Walsingham Shrine at Houghton St Giles. It was the final station chapel on the original pilgrim route to Walsingham. Charlotte set about the restoration of this chapel. A new statue of the Mother and Child was carved at Oberammagau based on the design of the original statue. This was possible due to the existence of a mediaeval seal of Walsingham Priory. In 1897 Pope Leo XIII re-established the restored fourteenth century slipper chapel as a Roman Catholic Shrine. This shrine is now known as the 'National Shrine of Our Lady of Walsingham'.

The restoration of the Roman Catholic Shrine of Our Lady of Walsingham was soon followed by the restoration of an Anglican Shrine dedicated to the same. One Fr Alfred Hope Patten SSC was appointed as the Church of England Vicar of Walsingham in 1921. He had a great interest in the pre-reformation pilgrimage to Walsingham and he decided to create a new statue of Our Lady of Walsingham based on the image depicted on the seal of the medieval priory. In 1922 the statue was set up in the Parish Church of St Mary attracting a great deal of interest and devotion amongst local people. This interest grew and eventually pilgrims from outside Walsingham once again began to make a pilgrimage to the site of the statue asking for the intercession of the Blessed Virgin Mary. This led to a place of hospitality being opened for pilgrims and eventually a new Holy House encased in a small pilgrimage church was dedicated and the statue was transferred there. This church was eventually enlarged to become the Anglican Shrine of Our Lady of Walsingham. There is now also a Christian Orthodox Church at Walsingham and this is known as the Orthodox Church of Saint Seraphim.

The restoration of veneration to Our Lady of Walsingham in the nineteenth and twentieth centuries was a very amazing thing bearing in mind that that the original Shrine of Our Lady of Walsingham had been destroyed in 1538. This restoration also meant that the vision of one very remarkable woman known as Richeldis continued to live on. Richeldis is a lost lady of mystery because the true identity of the visionary was lost to us perhaps due to the Norman Conquest and also due to the reformation. There were almost surely, prior to King Henry VIII's sacking of the monasteries, some detailed records about the visionary Richeldis and her origins. These would probably have been held by the Augustinian Canons at Walsingham. However, when Prior Vowell colluded with the King and agreed to the destruction of Walsingham's Shrine and Priory all records of this visionary would have been destroyed and the King would also have made sure no reference was made to her ever again. This was due to the fact that the shrine that had been created due to her vision was part of a past order of affairs which Henry VIII had destroyed. That shrine had been in the care of the Augustinian Canons. However, there were now no longer any monasteries or religious orders in England. Henry VIII had destroyed them all and taken both their land and their money. He did not wish any good record to remain about them because any good record might cause an insurrection. Therefore, all knowledge and detail of the visionary Richeldis was obliterated.

Who was this remarkable woman whose vision, over 950 years after its occurrence, still has some kind of strong influence on English spirituality? Her identity is disputed by academics and historians.

An authentic mid-twelfth-century charter in the Walsingham cartulary asserts that the original chapel was founded by Richeldis who was the widowed mother of a Geoffrey de Faverches. Therefore Dickinson (1956) argued that this Richeldis who was the Lady of Walsingham Manor in 1130 must be the foundress of the shrine. There is a problem with this theory however because the Pynson Ballad specifically states that the shrine was founded in 1061. Now while this Ballad was written at a much later date than the original shrine's foundation it is very odd that a date of 1061 is specifically mentioned in this document. There would appear to be no reason whatsoever for this date to have been made up or 'plucked out of a hat' as it were. Therefore, one can only assume that the shrine was indeed founded in 1061 and this foundation date was preserved and passed down in the oral tradition. However, if this is the case, Richeldis de Faverches could not have founded the Walsingham Shrine.

The historian Bill Flint (2014) argues that the term 'Richeldis' was not a name at all but a title given to the Lady of the

Manor. The title was likely to mean 'rich and fair' or 'rich and noble'. The idea that Richeldis is a title rather than a name could be supported by the fact that there is no such name as 'Richeldis' mentioned in the Domesday book. Flint refutes the later foundation date of the Shrine postulated by Dickinson and supports the date of 1061 given in the Pynson Ballad. Referring to the Little Domesday Book Flint argues that Queen Edith Swanneshals (the last Anglo-Saxon Queen of England) was the Lady of Walsingham Manor in 1061 and therefore the founder of the Walsingham Shrine. Flint states that Queen Edith, who is commonly known as 'Edith the Fair', was colloquially known as 'Richeldis' meaning 'rich and fair'. As the foundations of shrines usually precede the foundations of later priories on the same site Flint argues that the charter in the Walsingham cartulary refers to the later foundation of the Walsingham Priory. It has been argued by some scholars that Edith the Fair may be identical with Eadgifu the Fair who was one of the wealthiest magnates in England on the eve of the Norman Conquest. Queen Edith is believed to have fled England at the time of the conquest and to have lost all of her wealth. However, the problem with postulating Queen Edith as the founder of the shrine is that Queen Edith would not have been a widow in 1061 (seeing as her husband Harold Godwinson died in 1066) and the Pynson Ballad is very clear that the Walsingham shrine was founded by a 'noble widow' in 1061.

Unless any further documentation is discovered we are never likely to know for certain the true identity of the Walsingham visionary. It is unlikely that any further documentation about Richeldis will be discovered because much of it would probably have been destroyed in the Norman Conquest and anything remaining would certainly have been burnt during the reformation. The influence of this unknown widow has however been remarkable and her vision lives on today in the village of Walsingham. Richeldis was one of the earliest Marian visionaries and she was also probably a consecrated vowess. She would have been a woman of great influence and perhaps the last of the great Anglo-Saxon women of influence. Richeldis founded the Shrine in 1061 and the Norman Conquest soon followed in 1066.

Chapter Three

Virgins, Widows and Mystics

'Because I am a woman should I therefore believe that I ought not to tell you about the goodness of God since I saw at the same time that it is His will that it be known?'

Julian of Norwich

The earlier chapters have shown us the first phase of the English Catholic consecrated woman which was one of an extremely influential, noble and matriarchal figure. This figure was to completely disappear in the story of female consecrated spirituality in the English Catholic Church but this did not mean that women were to completely lose their influence in that church. New spheres of influence were to arise for Catholic consecrated women and this chapter looks at the second phase of female consecrated spirituality in Britain.

During the ninth century the double monasteries of men and women, which were often presided over by a matriarchal woman, were destroyed by the Danish raids and invasions. This persecution was so acute that by the end of the ninth century King Alfred of Wessex could comment on the total absence of the religious life. King Alfred tried to begin to rectify this and he founded two religious houses for women and one for men. However, it was not until the reign of King Edgar (959-973) that monasticism was fully revived and began to flourish. But this flourishing would not last for very long in its late Anglo-Saxon form because, of course, in 1066 there was the Norman Conquest. The last Anglo-Saxon King, Harold Godwinson, was defeated at the Battle of Hastings and his death marked the end of Anglo-Saxon rule over England. This had a disastrous effect on the English nobility who, in the main, controlled the governance of ecclesiastical institutions at that time. This governance was gradually taken from the English and given to officials from the continent and, as has already been noted in chapter two, may have been a factor in the removal from records of the name of the original visionary of the Walsingham message. The Walsingham Shrine is traditionally believed to have been erected five years before the Norman Conquest. For all these reasons female Catholic consecrated life underwent a major upheaval during this period and changed significantly. The matriarchal woman was gone and when female consecrated life again began to emerge in England it emerged under a new form and this was the form of the anchoress. Anchoresses appear to have been both virgins and widows and they lived in cells attached to churches. However, there is also evidence that the specific vocation of the consecrated widow, who remained at home rather than in a cell, also survived and continued during this time. Consecrated widows were known as 'vowesses' and they were usually fairly well-off women in society who placed their wealth and property at the service of others.

In regards to the anchorite movement – this movement had its roots established in very early Christianity with St Thecla of Iconium. Thecla was said to have been converted by St Paul himself. She refused her parents' wishes that she marry in order to follow St Paul and as a result of this was sent to the amphitheatre to be eaten by beasts. Thecla managed to escape before the beasts attacked her and she then retired to live as an anchorite in a cave for 72 years. This kind of withdrawal, as portrayed by Thecla herself, became widespread in the late third century and arrived in Britain in the early seventh century. It achieved the height of its prominence in England in the fourteenth century with Julian of Norwich. It would appear that the reason for this flourishing of the anchorite movement in England at that time was the decimation of the established Anglo-Saxon religious life during the Danish raids and the later Norman Conquest. As the religious communities had been destroyed the only path left open for fervent female spiritual women was the path of isolation. Thompson (1991) states that many of the religious communities of the early middle ages grew up around an anchoress. This would suggest that anchoresses appeared to eventually provide the focal point for a new form of female community religious life. Their call to the solitary life seemed to be the initial impulse for many cells which later developed into nunneries. However, before looking at the nunneries that developed around them, it is necessary to examine anchoresses in their own right.

During the twelfth and thirteenth century there were apparently around 123 women living the life of anchoresses in England and eventually a rule was written for them. This rule is known as the 'Ancrene Riwle' of 1229 or 'Ancrene Wisse' and the author of this rule is unknown. Ancrene Wisse was originally composed for three sisters who chose to become anchoresses. The work consists of eight parts. Parts 1 and 8 consist of what is called the 'Outer Rule' which relates to the anchoresses' exterior life. Parts 2-7 consist of the 'Inner Rule' which relates to the anchoresses' interior life. The writer of this rule illustrates the ascetism of the anchoresses and also gives us an insight into their lives. The author reprimands the anchoresses for fasting on bread and water too often; tells them to wear no iron, haircloth or hedgehog skins and also advises them not to beat themselves without leave of their confessors. In the Outer Rule anchoresses are also advised not to possess any beast except a cat and due to this it is believed that the ownership of cats by anchoresses was widespread. For this reason, Julian of Norwich, who was England's most renowned anchoress in the Early Middle Ages, is often portrayed in iconography together with a cat.

Julian of Norwich is the most famous of the English anchoresses mainly because of her book,' The Revelations of Divine Love' which was the first book of any sort to be written in English by a woman. However, before examining Julian's achievements it should also be remembered that there were many other earlier female anchoresses (pre-Julian) living the anchorite way of life. It was around this earlier group of anchoresses that communities of nuns may have originally developed. One of the earliest of these was Christina of Markyate.

Christina was born with the name of Theodora (Greek for gift of God) at around 1097. She had come from a wealthy Anglo-Saxon family who were trying to accommodate the Normans at the time. As a child Christina is said to have talked to Christ, 'as if he were a man whom she could see'. She became friends with an older man named Sueno and he became her first mentor or spiritual director. Apparently Sueno had once lived an unholy life and it is believed that Christina's faith renewed his and so they helped each other. Christina visited St. Alban's Abbey as a teenager and apparently had some kind of spiritual experience at this time. This experience led her to make a private vow of chastity about which she told Sueno and no one else. Sometime later, while visiting an aunt named Elfgifu, Christina met Bishop Ranulf Flambard. Her aunt was apparently his mistress and the mother of at least two of his sons. It was alleged that this bishop also tried to seduce Christina in 1114 but she spurned and rebuffed him. Apparently due to this he then tried to exact his revenge by arranging a marriage for her with a young nobleman named Beorhtred. Christina's parents were happy for this marriage to take place but she was not. As word went around about her plight an elderly hermit named Eadwine came to her rescue. Christina escaped dressed in men's clothes and Eadwine took her to stay with an anchoress at Flamstead named Alfwen. It was apparently at this time that Christina (who had originally been named Theodora) changed her name. The name Christina in the Greek actually means 'little Christ'.

Following her change of name Christina was next assisted by a hermit and sub-deacon of St Alban's Abbey whose cell was at Markyate. After two years Christina was released from the marriage contract that had been arranged by her parents and she was able to come out of hiding. Following the death of the elderly hermit who had assisted her Christina took over his hermitage near St. Alban's Abbey. Other women joined her there and she eventually took her vows at St Alban's Abbey in 1131. She later established Markyate Priory in 1145 and became a prioress. Christina had a close relationship of mutual support with the Abbot of St Albans for many years and it is believed that he altered the St Albans Psalter as a gift to her. Apparently an illuminated 'C' was placed at the beginning of Psalm 105.

Christina's story clearly illustrates how communities of nuns began to develop around anchoresses and how the anchorite movement eventually provided a focal point for new forms of female community religious life. However, the anchorite movement, in its own right, became famous during the early and high Middle Ages. Anchoresses lived in a simple cell which was attached to the walls of the local village church. Examples of an anchorite cell remain in England and one of the best examples is at St Mary and St Cuthbert Church in Chester-le-Street. It had a small window through which viewing the altar and joining in the sacrificial prayer of the Mass was possible in the common wall facing the sanctuary. Anchoresses would also provide spiritual advice to visitors through this window as they gained a great reputation for wisdom. They provided a spiritual and geographical focus for many people in their community and wider society and thus were very influential. They were at the very centre of their communities and it can certainly be argued that their influence and reputation was probably as great, if not greater, than the influence of the priest to whose church they were attached. The majority of anchorites in England were female anchoresses although there were some male anchorites. The most famous of the female anchoresses is Julian of Norwich.

Molinari dates Julian's birth at around 1342 but apart from this very little is known of her life. Even her true name is unknown as the name 'Julian' by which history commonly describes her derives from the fact that her anchoress's cell was built onto the wall of the Church of St Julian in Norwich. It was common at that time for anchoresses to take the name of the church to which they were attached. The fact that Julian's anchorold was at St Julian's Church, Conisford, Norwich is established by three wills dated 1404, 1415 and 1416. This anchorold belonged to the Benedictine monastery at Carrow and due to this there has been speculation that Julian herself may have originally been an enclosed Benedictine nun. However, it is not known whether she actually belonged to the Benedictine community or was simply a recluse living in the grounds. Today the consensus by scholars seems to be that she was a widowed lay woman who became an anchoress (and would have been consecrated a widow/anchoress by the Bishop of Norwich) after her visions. These visions occurred when she was seriously ill and at death's door and prompted her to write her book '*Revelations of Divine Love*' after her recovery. In the earlier version of this book Julian describes her illness and who she sent for. Upjohn (1989) states that it is significant that while she was ill she did not send for 'my priest' but for 'the parson, my curate, to be at my end. He came with a little boy and brought a cross'. Upjohn also goes on to state that she finds it significant that Julian's mother was present during this illness rather than any abbess. It is also possible that this illness may have been the plague and that Julian may have lost her husband to the same illness while she survived.

Upjohn uses the work of Sr. Benedicta Ward and Kenneth Leech (Julian Reconsidered 1988) to state her case against Julian having ever been an enclosed nun. In this work they argue that Julian's writings bear no mark of the cloister. She is never mentioned in any existing records of Carrow Priory or any other nunnery. She never refers to her fellow sisters and all her concerns are for 'mine even-Christians' i.e., lay folk. They also argue that had she been an enclosed nun, a nunnery with such an outstanding member would have ensured that she was buried in their grounds and made sure that many copies of her book were available. The problem with this argument, however, is that during the Reformation all records in regards to the religious life were burnt and destroyed. In addition to this, most religious houses were also looted and destroyed or ransacked and then given to King Henry VIII's conspirators. It is therefore not surprising that it is not known where Julian was buried or that virtually all copies of her book were destroyed at that time. So, it is possible that she could originally have been an enclosed nun although more likely, due to her style of writing, that she was a lay person who later became a consecrated widow in the form of an anchoress. Regardless of her status only a few copies of her book have survived.

Julian of Norwich's book *'Revelations of Divine Love'* is believed to be the first book written in English by a woman. There are two versions of this book which are the short text and the long text. The short text survives in only one manuscript which is the mid-fifteenth century Amherst Manuscript. This was copied from the original in Julian's lifetime in 1413. The long text survives in several versions. One version is known as the *Paris Manuscript* and was produced by English Benedictine nuns in exile in the Antwerp region. The other versions are now in the British Library's Sloane Collection. These were written out and preserved in the Cambrai and Paris houses of the English Benedictine nuns in exile in the mid-17th century following the reformation and the establishment of Protestantism in England under Elizabeth I. The fact that Benedictine nuns saved this manuscript does not necessarily mean that Julian had been an enclosed nun although she may have been a nun just as she may have been a lay person who became a consecrated widow under vow. However, she certainly had strong ties with the Benedictines regardless of whether she was a consecrated widow or an enclosed nun.

In modern times the world-wide Church seems to have, in the main, lost the idea that widows and virgins can consecrate their lives singly to God and take vows of chastity while living in the world. Nevertheless, in recent years there are beginnings of a revival of this vocation. In Julian's time, however, single consecration by vow was common practice in England particularly amongst widows. Consecrated widows, known as vowesses, lived independently in secular residences. Vowesses initiated a new spiritual life for themselves after the deaths of their husbands while also maintaining control of their money and resources which they often used for charitable purposes. There are many references to vowesses in English manuscripts dating from the eighth century right through to the sixteenth century. Canon Law required the bishop to complete the vowing rituals and the vowess donned a mantle, veil and ring all blessed by the bishop. Thus, the idea of women consecrating their lives singly to God was common in Julian's time and taking vows as a widow to become an anchoress, rather than a vowess, would have probably been completely natural to her.

In her book 'The Revelations of Divine Love' Julian describes a series of visions which she experienced after an illness which may have been the plague. The first version of this book was written shortly after her recovery from her illness while the second version of this book was written some twenty years later. Molinari states that the second version is the most definitive as it describes what Julian felt about her visions after twenty years of reflection, thought and prayer. This second version of Julian's book has also led to her being regarded as one of the greatest Christian mystics of all time.

Mysticism is a form of spirituality which is concerned with the pursuit of perfection and union with the Absolute and it can also be found in Eastern religions such as Buddhism and Islam as well as Christianity. Julian was not unique in her times in being a Christian mystic. There were also other famous Christian mystics including: Walter Hilton; the unknown author of the Cloud of unknowing; Ramon Lull; Richard Rolle and Margery Kempe. However, Julian's teaching on mysticism differed from that of her

contemporaries and it is probably due to this that she has
become renowned.

The mystical path within the Eastern religions was (and
remains today) in many ways a path of negation and the
mystical path of Christianity during Julian's time was very
similar. In fact, it could be argued that Christian mysticism
followed the way of negation even more rigorously than the
mysticism of the East. However, Julian was not a follower of
the negative path. Early Christian martyrs such as Ignatius of
Antioch had readily accepted and almost sought out
martyrdom as a way of uniting with God. Other European
Christian mystics who were contemporary with Julian, such
as Saint Catherine of Siena, longed for death and martyrdom
believing this to be the ultimate Christian crown. However,
Julian, while ill, had no such desire. She wrote:

I was right sorry and loathe to die though not for anything
that I was afeared for; for I trusted in God. But it was because
I would have lived on to have loved God better and for a
longer time - that I might, by the grace of that living, have the
more knowing and love of God in the bliss of heaven

Julian's mysticism does not involve negativism and severe
mortifications in order to achieve union with the Divine or
the Absolute. Instead, she teaches the 'second conversion
'and the possibility of uniting fully with God in this world
rather than the next. Man or woman, moved by grace, sees
the desire of his/her grace and begins to desire the Absolute
fervently. This desire for God leads to the mystical life which
Julian sees as having three stages. The first stage is longing

for God, the second is uniting with God and the last is beholding. Beholding can probably be seen as the equivalent of St. Thomas Aquinas' 'Beatific Vision'. It means being so absorbed in God that nothing, other than the Absolute itself, has significance. An individual's whole life is directed towards the force of love which has possessed this individual. This love has totally taken hold of the individual and nothing other than this love is acceptable as a mode of living. Once one has tasted the love of God one cannot resist. The full union with God will follow and it will be achieved through the total submission of an individual's will to the will of God through the experience of prayer. Prayer is always crucial in Julian's teaching. It is a response to the call of God and involves a relationship between the human being and God.

Julian was a unique and independent woman who created a new mystical theology that proposed a completely new and different mystical path. Julian also spoke of the 'motherhood of God' and with this concept she was again breaking new ground. St Anselm had first fermented the idea of the motherhood of God with his teaching that Christ gave birth to the human person by his dying on the cross and bringing the human person to new life. However, this idea of the motherhood of God had never really been developed in Christianity prior to Julian and has not since been developed in any great detail following her passing. Julian writes:

I understood three manners of beholding of motherhood in God; the first is grounded in our kind making; the second is taking of our kind – and there beginneth the motherhood of Grace; the third is motherhood of working – and therein is a

*forthspreading of the same Grace, of length and breadth and
of height and of deepness without end.*

Later Julian writes of the love of God as feminine
motherhood as follows:

*The kind loving mother that witteth and knoweth the need of
her child, she keepeth it full tenderly as the kind and condition
of motherhood will.*

Julian's feminist doctrine was almost certainly not disagreed
with by the English Church of her day. We can discern this
because Julian was highly regarded in her times and her
counsel was sought out by many from far and wide. The fact
that it was not disputed is interesting because it would
suggest that there was still an element of matriarchal
thinking in England which had not completely died out
following the Danish raids and the end of the Anglo-Saxon
period. It is known that this anchoress was highly regarded
from the autobiography of Margery Kempe, a married female
mystic, whose writings also survive to this day. Margery
narrates how she paid a visit to Julian in search of spiritual
direction. This was due to the fact that the wisdom of Julian
was very well-known and acclaimed in her day. The
anchoresses of Julian's time may have lived alone in a cell but
they were certainly not isolated. They appeared to have a
Christian ministry of giving spiritual direction to lay people
who visited them.

Following the rediscovery and recognition of the female
vocation due to the anchorite movement there was again a

resurgence of female spirituality and the female community religious life in England was re-created. Many new nunneries were founded and a great many of these had their roots in the anchorite movement and began with women who were previously anchoresses. However, it should be pointed out that in these new religious houses which were founded in Mediaeval England, female nuns had nowhere near the influence that previous consecrated women had experienced in Anglo Saxon England. These women were not matriarchs. They were simply enclosed nuns. They also did not attend councils of the church in a position of influence like Hilda of Whitby and others had done. The influence of women in the English church did seem to be declining and in the main these new religious houses for women were founded by men.

Sempringham Priory was a Priory in Lincolnshire and this Priory was built by St Gilbert of Sempringham. St Gilbert established the Gilbertine Order in 1131 by inducting a number of women in his parish who were anchoresses but now wished to live a communal enclosed life. Gilbert built a cell for these women attached to his church and this marked the beginning of the Gilbertine order which became famed prior to the reformation. The early rule was based on the rule of St. Benedict but Gilbert soon realised that if the nuns were to remain enclosed, they would need to be served by others. As a result of this he placed some village girls under a simple vow to fetch and carry for the nuns. This decision of his may very well have marked the beginning of what is now known as 'Third Order' in England. Members of 'Third Orders' today are associates of various religious orders. Third Order members are usually single or married people who wish, in addition to their commitment to marriage, to make another commitment to follow God as much as possible in their lay state. In regards to Sempringham, this Order continued to spread and in order to safeguard its possessions regular labour was needed and this led to lay brothers been added to the movement. Augustinian Canons were later added to govern the women and Sempringham became a double monastery. However, it is important to note that this double monastery bore no resemblance to the double monasteries of the Anglo-Saxon period. During that period double monasteries were, in the main, presided over by matriarchal women. In this case it was the men who governed the Order while the women were its backbone. These women were still, of course, influential but their influence was not in any way on a par with the influence that women had previously had in Anglo Saxon England. Sempringham became a priory around 1139 and it was at this time that an associated house near Sleaford was established. By the time Gilbert died there were nine double monasteries established and his order had achieved wide renown. This Order was sadly completely destroyed at a later date by King Henry VIII at the time of the English reformation.

In addition to the anchorite movement which led to the foundation of nunneries and also to the foundation of Sempringham some Norman monasteries were granted land in England due to the fact that the Norman Conquest had intensified links between English and continental monasteries. Some monasteries in England were linked with great reform movements overseas such as Fontevrault and this led to religious houses being founded in this country which were dependent on a Mother House overseas.

Fontevrault was founded by Robert of Arbrissel and it was, from the time of its very origin, concerned with the female vocation and ministry. The Order bore the name of the Mother House where in the beginning Robert's concern for women led him to found a monastery for their special care. Robert included men in his Order but they were subservient to women and he chose a widow, Petronella, as Abbess in the village of Fontevrault near Chinon in Anjou France. The Order was composed of double monasteries in which the community consisted of both men and women, in separate quarters of the abbey, all of whom were subject to the Abbess of Fontevrault. The Abbey of Fontevrault itself consisted of four separate communities all completely managed by the same abbess. In this regard the French Order of Fontevrault was very similar to the double monasteries which had existed in England at an earlier date. The order spread to England and three nunneries were founded. These were at Westwood, Nuneaton and Amesbury. However, these were nunneries and not double monasteries. In England women did not enjoy the same prestige and influence at these outposts of Fontevrault that women enjoyed at the original foundation. However, Fontevrault did become greatly favoured by the English royal houses and its benefactor was Eleanor of Aquitane who was eventually buried at the Mother House with her husband Henry II. Due to the dissolution of religious orders at the time of the reformation little is known of the English women who joined the outposts of this French Order. However, the name of the town Nun-Eaton still bears witness to their existence at that place in earlier times.

Fontevrault is one example of a continental Order which established nunneries in England in the earlier period of the Middle Ages but there were also others. These were Orders such as Cluny, Citeaux, Arrouaise and Premonte. Of the Order of Cluny two nunneries were founded in England which are usually described as Cluniac and these were the Abbey of Delapre and the Priory of Arthington. The twelfth century reformed congregations of Augustinian Canons such as the Preonstratensian and Arousian Orders also initially welcomed women but later excluded them. The reverse was true of the Cistercians who initially were very hostile to women but later welcomed them. A decree was initially passed to stop the Cistercians concerning themselves with women religious but by the mid thirteenth century this was overturned. Over 27 nunneries originated from or became Cistercian. The most famous of these were Marham and Tarrant.

The continental Orders were instrumental in the foundation of nunneries in early mediaeval England but there was also one other way in which nunneries may have been founded at this time and this is through the hospitals. Thompson states that hospitals were often religious houses and the distinction between hospitals and priories was one of degree rather than of kind. If that is the case then the active religious life may have existed in England far earlier than generally supposed. Following the demise of the double monasteries where women were certainly influential in the country and the world in an intellectual way, it has generally been believed that that when nunneries were re-founded women in England were enclosed. However, Thompson believes mediaeval hospitals were concerned with both the soul and the body and she quotes St Mary de Pre as an example of a hospital for sick women which later developed into a priory. Another example of a nunnery which was also a hospital was the nunnery dedicated to St. Mary Magdalene founded on St. Michael's Hill, Bristol by Eva Fitz Harding. Charter evidence confirms the existence of Eva and documents also refer to the hospital of St Mary Magdalene.

This chapter has thus examined the second phase or sphere of English Catholic women during the post Norman Conquest and early Middle Ages period. It has been established that the anchorite movement was very important during this period. Anchoresses were highly influential women in their own right and they were viewed as spiritual directors or counsellors whose help and discernment was sought by the populace in times of trouble. Anchoresses were also instrumental in the founding of new religious houses for women in England during this period. However other religious houses for women in England were also established by continental religious orders. Consecrated widows, who were known as vowesses, were also important during this period. All the above women were both consecrated and celibate. However, while consecrated female celibacy is the main topic of this book it would not be right to close this chapter without mentioning Margery Kempe who was a married female mystic.

The Book of Margery Kempe is the earliest surviving autobiographical writing in English and it was lost for centuries. In 1934 a fifteenth century manuscript came to light. This manuscript had for a long time been in the possession of an ancient Catholic family, the Butler-Bowdons. Margery herself could not read or write and she initially employed a scribe to write her book but this first attempt failed. She then, in 1436, persuaded a local priest to write her autobiography and this second attempt succeeded. The book was then written and despite the later reformation a copy of it survived.

At the beginning of her book Margery relates the demonic torment she experienced after her first pregnancy. She states this torment only ceased after she experienced a vision of Christ. Today she would probably be considered as having suffered from postnatal depression. However, her vision of Christ appeared to help her overcome this illness. Margery then went into business and attempted to run both a brewery and a grain mill but both her businesses failed. She wanted to be more devout but was tempted by sexual pleasures and social climbing for some years. Eventually Margery dedicated herself completely to the spiritual calling that she felt her earlier vision had demanded and she negotiated a chaste relationship with her husband.
After this Margery entered on a life of pilgrimage and of travel which was extremely remarkable for a woman in her day bearing in mind how difficult travel was then. Margery was from King's Lynn in Norfolk (then called Bishop's Lynn) but her pilgrimages took her far beyond British horizons to the Holy Land, Assisi, Santiago de Compostela and Rome. This

was highly impressive for a woman of her times when travel was much riskier and more turbulent than it is today. Margery was also arrested several times during her lifetime and she was subject to examinations to establish whether or not she was a heretic. It appears that Margery was suspected of having ties with the Lollards (who were regarded as heretical) but was later exonerated of having such ties. Margery's book details her domestic tribulations; her extensive pilgrimages and her conversations with God. She is also one of the few sources that give us details of the female mystic and anchorite Julian of Norwich who is described above. Margery visited Julian in 1413. Today Margery is honoured in the Anglican Communion but she has never been declared a Catholic saint.

The post Anglo-Saxon period which leads into the early and later Middle-Ages shows a lot of healthy activity in regards to female spirituality within the English Catholic Church during these times. This activity includes the anchorite movement which appears to have culminated in the example of Julian of Norwich; the founding of new forms of religious life for women by anchoresses and by the continental orders and the continuing of the singly vowed life, for widows in particular, in the form of vowesses. All of these examples of female spirituality must have been very exciting during their time. However, the question still remains as to whether women held the same influence in medieval England as they had previously held in Anglo Saxon England prior to the Norman Conquest. If influence is regarded as power then the answer to this question is almost certainly negative. By this time the powerful influence of women was definitely on the decline. This is because English women, unlike their Anglo-Saxon Forebears, no longer participated in the councils of the church. English women, in the main, also no longer presided over double monasteries. However, if influence is regarded as being held as a great spiritual example by one's contemporaries and peers then it can certainly be argued that Julian of Norwich achieved such influence.

Chapter Four

Pre-Reformation Decline and Post Reformation Exile

'Let your vocation be constant, efficacious and affectionate' –
Mary Ward

The Early Middle Ages, which had produced influential
consecrated women such as Christina of Markyate and Julian
of Norwich and also many singly vowed women who were
known as vowesses, had been a good time spiritually for
women in the English Catholic Church but unfortunately this
was not to continue. The later Middle Ages was to see a
decline in female vocations in two main ways. Firstly, there
was a decline in the number of women taking vows as
anchoresses and vowesses although both vocations did
continue right up until the reformation. Secondly, in regards
to enclosed consecrated women, there was a change in the
way some religious women viewed their vocation and this
damaged their reputation. Chaucer, writing in the late
fourteenth century, gives us a picture of a prioress that
differs starkly from the earlier picture of Christina of
Markyate.

Ther was also a Nonne, a Prioresse

That of hir smyling was ful simple and coy;

Hire greatteste ooth was but by Seint Loy,

And she was cleped madame Eglentyne.

Ful weel she soong the service dyvyne

Entuned in hir nose ful seemly;

And Frenssh she spak ful faire and fetisly,

After the scole of Stratford-atte-Bowe,

For Frenssh of Parys was to hire unknown.

At mete wel y-taught was she with-alle;

She leet no morsel from hir lippes falle,

Ne wette hir fyngres in hir sauce depe.

Wel koude she carie a morsel and wel kepe,

That no drope ne fille upon hir breste;

In curteisie was set ful muchel hir leste.

Hire over-lippe wiped she so clene

That in hir coppe ther was no ferthyng sene

Of grese, when she drunken hadde hir draughte;

Ful seemly after hir mete she raughte.

And sikerly she was of greet desporte,

And ful plesaunt and amayble of port;

And peyned hire to countrfete cheere

Of court, and been estatlich of manere,

And to ben holden digne of reverence.

But for to speken of hire conscience,

She was so charitable and so pitous

She wolde wepe, if that she saugh a mous

Kaught in a trappe, if it were deed or bedde.

Of smale houndes hadde she that she fedde

With rosted flesh, or milk and wastrel breed;

But soore wept she if oon of hem were deed,

Or if men smoot it with a yerde smerte

And al was conscience and tender herte.

Ful semyly hir wympul pynched was;

Hire nose tretys, hr eyen greye as glas,

Hir mouth ful small and ther-to softe and reed;

But sikerly she hadde a fair forheed;

It was almost a spanne brood I trowe;

For, hardily, she was nat undergrowe.

Ful fetys was hir cloke, as I was war;

Of small coral aboute hire arm she bar

A paire of bedes, gauded al with grene,

And ther-on heng a brooch of gold ful sheene,

On which ther was first write a crowned A,

And after Amor vincet Omnia.

The main point in Chaucer's description of the Prioress is to illustrate how she dressed in high fashion and presented herself more in the way of a noble lady at court than an enclosed nun. The wide forehead was regarded as a sign of beauty during these times and we are also told that the prioress's mouth was soft and red. She swears by St Loy and Pollard (1976) states there has been much discussion as to why the Prioress pictured here should swear by St Loy since St Loy had refused to take an oath even when pressed to do so by King Dagobert. Pollard comes to the conclusion that the nun did not swear at all but another more likely explanation is surely that Chaucer is making fun of the nun or ridiculing her. He could mean of course that any oaths she made or had made would mean nothing to her. Another possibility is that the reference to St Loy might be a hint that the prioress was empty headed and not well- learned and therefore swore by a saint who refused to ever take an oath. Chaucer certainly satirises the nun's learning for example when he writes of her English spoken French which she learnt at Stratford-atte-Bowe.

The prioress is called 'Madame' because this was the common title of the day which was given to all nuns after their consecration. It represented their marriage to Christ and can be clearly seen in the Lincoln Order for consecrating nuns written about 1480. Here the Bishop states:

Dowghters and virgyns, now that ye are maryed and despowed to hym that is above Kyng and Kaysor, unto Iesu Cryste, mete it is and so must you from hensforth yn token of the same be callyd Madame and Ladye.

The prioress is also very concerned with her appearance and Power states that the nun's revealing of her high forehead showed her concern for modern fashions. High foreheads were the height of fashion and Power illustrates this with the accusations which were brought against Clemence Medforde Prioresse of Ankerwyke in 1441

The Prioresse wears golden rings and she carries her veil too high above her forehead.

Chaucer's nun thus appears to be rather worldly as she was clearly concerned with her appearance. She also appears to have various affectations. This can be seen from Chaucer's descriptions of her at mealtimes where she is portrayed as having the most exemplary manners. Of course, there was nothing at all wrong with good manners. The practice of good manners and courtesy by all made everyone's life much more pleasant. However, one gets the impression that what Chaucer is trying to say with this description of the nun's behaviour at mealtimes is that she was very affectatious and behaved like a courtly lady rather than a woman of the cloister. Certainly, at this time the religious life had become much laxer. Many nuns no longer lived strict, ascetic lives and there was carelessness in the performance of the monastic hours, gay clothes, the keeping of pet animals, dancing, games and gossip. Today we would see nothing wrong with a consecrated woman living in the world wearing ordinary clothes or keeping a pet and no doubt at this time consecrated widows did this to some degree. The point here however is that the nun concerned was meant to be an enclosed nun and she was clearly not following the rule of her day. Even consecrated widows, who were living in the world and known as vowesses, were expected to wear a cloak, a mantle and a ring but this nun was dressing in the height of fashion. Nuns also did not follow the strict rules of enclosure which officially remained canon law and this can be seen in the fact that this nun was on her way to Canterbury.

In 1299 Pope Boniface VIII had issued the Bull Penculoso which stated that nuns should be strictly enclosed and remain always in their cells. Even pilgrimages were not encouraged and the earlier Council of York had stated: 'In order that the opportunity of wandering about may be taken from them we forbid them to take the road of pilgrimage.'

However, during the late Middle Ages these rules were continuously flouted as were other rules which stated that nuns must obtain the permission of the head before talking with visitors and all such meetings must take place in the parlour in the hearing of another nun. This did not happen in practice and seculars often slept overnight. There were also other lax practices such as the breaking of the rule of silence. Perhaps due to the undisciplined lives led by many nuns in the late Middle Ages there was a decline in vocations to the female enclosed religious life. In the period prior to the reformation there were only 138 nunneries excluding double houses and of these only four had more than thirty inmates. The proportion of women who became nuns was very small compared to the total female population and while this may always be expected to be the case, in the later Middle Ages the number of vocations had reached a particularly low ebb. The reasons for taking the veil were also on occasions dubious. There were some women who entered convents with real spirits of devotion but there were others who entered purely because the convent offered an honourable alternative to marriage for aristocratic ladies whose families had been unable to find them a spouse. There were also girls who were thrust unwillingly into the convent and these were often children whose parents had decided on the religious life as a career for them. For girls such as these the convent became a form of prison and the unwilling nun bore no resemblance to the earlier figure of Christina of Markyate who had disobeyed and abandoned family for the ascetic life. While there were men who also entered the religious life without a vocation Power states that there were a larger number of women who did the same. This was due to the fact that there was hardly any other available career for unmarried ladies of noble birth. The mediaeval literature of the time was full of stories of nuns running away for love and this would seem to indicate that it was well known that many of the women behind the veils wore those veils unwillingly. The nun was seen as a lovebird beating her wings against the bars of her cage and Power cites the following poem as an example

The nun is complaining,
Her tears down raining,

She sobbeth and sigheth,
To her sisters she crieth:
Misery me!

O what can be worse than this
Life that I dree,
When naughty and lovelorn
And wanten I be.

All the night long I unwillingly wake
How gladly a lad in mine arms would I take.

Not only does this poem illustrate the fact that many nuns were reluctant enclosed celibate women but it also illustrates the mood of the age and would seem to suggest that ascetism was no longer an ideal. Romantic love now seemed to be the desire of most young women and the idea of the religious vocation as a vocation of high romance was an age away from this period. Enclosed nuns no longer lived ascetic lives or lives of particular sacrifice and many heads of houses lived in great luxury and enjoyed great freedom of movement. There appeared in some cases to be very little difference between the life of the female 'enclosed' religious and the life of her middle class or aristocratic contemporaries. Perhaps because 'enclosed' nuns lived similar lives to those of their secular contemporaries their 'raison d'etre' was called into question and this may have been one of the reasons for the decline in vocations at the time. However, the fact is that every age will always have different expectations of its spiritual or religious women. Therefore, the most important thing in any age is that the women involved in ministry can reach out and touch the people they wish to minister to by their personal examples of faith. This was clearly not happening in the late Middle Ages and there appeared to be some disillusionment with the female 'enclosed' religious of the day due to the fact that they behaved like women at court. The point to note here is that the female 'enclosed' religious woman was not at this time connecting with the people to whom she was ministering. There were not droves of people relying on her prayers.

The female ministry had been diminished and by the time of the late Middle Ages the anchoresses were beginning to die out along with the vowesses and the female enclosed religious nuns. This was a period of great darkness for female consecrated spirituality but even in this period there remained some women who resolutely followed their star despite the mores of the times. These women who held on to their vision despite the difficulties of their times included both consecrated women in Syon and consecrated vowesses some of whom were in some way attached to Syon.

Syon was the only Bridgettine house in England and it was also a double monastery. The first stone of this monastery was laid by King Henry V on 22 February 1415. The Bridgettine Order was a modified Order of St. Augustine with particular devotions to the passion of Christ and the honour of the Virgin Mary. The King's original foundation consisted of 85 persons and these were: one Abbess; 59 nuns; one Confessor General; 12 priests; four deacons and eight lay brethren.

The order grew and became extremely wealthy. Its net income far exceeded that of any other nunnery. The nuns of Syon also practised very good observance unlike many of their contemporaries in other houses and they had an informed devotional life which was based on the English mystics of the earlier 1300s. Learning was another attribute of the Syon nuns and the monastery had a magnificent library and was renowned for its intellectual distinction. The monastery did not suffer from the crisis of vocations that affected other religious houses and it housed over 60 nuns. Many of these nuns came from well-known families and had aristocratic connections. Also attached to Syon in a looser way were many vowesses or consecrated widows. These were the women, mentioned in previous chapters, who took vows of chastity without the accompanying monastic vows of poverty and obedience. They were free to own their own property and to live where they chose but they often chose to live near a large and active monastery. Syon was a Catholic beacon of light in troublesome times and not surprisingly, bearing in mind its elevated status, there was strong opposition from Syon at the time of the reformation.

At the time of the dissolution Syon Abbey was the wealthiest convent in England in the sense that the other nunneries were regarded as insignificant. Syon, however, was different to the other convents because it was not strictly speaking a convent at all. It was a double monastery and a throwback to the earlier Anglo-Saxon times. This abbey had always been presided over by an abbess and by the time of the Reformation there had been eight abbesses. The last abbess was Agnes Jordan (1520 – 1539). The legal corporate identity of Syon was 'The Abbess and Convent' which could transact business by affixing its single corporate seal. The convent (from Latin convenio – come together) consisted of the abbess and nuns together with the confessor and all religious men. The abbess was the overall presiding officer. In the case of Agnes Jordan, she was therefore the last bastion of female authority in the English Catholic Church. Bearing in mind that Henry VIII was one of the greatest sexist despots in English history it is hardly surprising that Syon did not survive.

At the time of the reformation there was strong opposition from the Order of Syon and many refused to acknowledge the King's new title. However, the opposition was stronger on the male side of the Order than on the female side. The monastery was thus one of the few in England that struggled long in the clutch of circumstance before giving a reluctant consent and some of its members and associates were martyred. One particular monk named Richard Reynolds arranged a meeting between Sir Thomas More and Elizabeth Barton. Sir Thomas More was the King's chief opponent at the time of the reformation and Elizabeth Barton was a Benedictine nun who also strongly opposed the reformation. All these three individuals were eventually executed by Henry VIII for their opposition to the reformation but the last Abbess of Syon survived. It seems that initially she had capitulated because she had thought that King Henry VIII would allow the monastery to continue under new governance. When this proved not to be the case, she retired graciously to the Manor House of Southlands in Buckinghamshire and received a pension of £200 a year. However, when the monastery did surrender in 1539 the abbess did not take her fellow sisters with her. A large number of them clearly resisted and the community was expelled. This expelled community exiled itself to the Netherlands. The community did return again to England briefly during the reign of the Catholic Mary Tudor but was then again later expelled under Elizabeth I. On this occasion the community went to Portugal in exile and remained there until their final return to England in 1861. The Syon community was therefore the only English religious community that survived the reformation unbroken.

Syon had struggled hard during the reformation before its final and reluctant consent but the majority of nunneries were regarded as insignificant at that time. This was almost certainly one of the factors that allowed Henry VIII to destroy them along with the male monasteries. The causes of the English reformation are vast and complex but what is certain is the fact that Henry's desire for an annulment played a crucial role in the events that led to the dissolution of the monasteries. In order to understand the driving force behind Henry VIII's actions it is necessary to be aware of Catholic teaching on marriage which has changed very little until this day.

It is commonly stated that the English reformation and the dissolution of the monasteries happened because Henry VIII wanted 'a divorce' but this is not strictly true. At the time Henry was Catholic in his thinking and it was an annulment he sought rather than a divorce. An annulment, in Catholic teaching, is a declaration that a marriage which was solemnised in the Church as a marriage was in fact not a marriage and is therefore null and void. An annulment is not a divorce because a divorce, according to Catholic teaching, is the ending of a valid and true marriage where as an annulment states that no true marriage ever took place. The marriage was invalid. There can be many reasons why the Catholic Church may declare a marriage null and void such as a failure to consummate the marriage or a failure to consent to a marriage. In regards to invalid consent this may be because either or both of the parties may have believed themselves to have been forced into the marriage by others due to social or political reasons. A marriage could also be annulled because the parties concerned were very immature at the time of the marriage and did not really understand the level of commitment that was required of them. In Henry's case he argued that his marriage to Catherine of Aragon was not valid because he had been forced into the marriage by others for political reasons. Henry had married his deceased brother's wife and he stated that there had been inexplicit pressure on him to do the same. He tried to use a passage from the Bible in Leviticus to support the case that his marriage had been invalid. He stated that this marriage was invalid and he wanted to contract a 'true' marriage with Anne Boleyn. While Henry stated that he believed that there was something wrong with his first marriage and that this had led him to produce no male heirs, it is also clear that King Henry was very infatuated with Anne Boleyn and this infatuation was a driving force in his attempts to secure an annulment.

Henry VIII first raised the question of his marriage with Rome in 1527. At this time, he remained very Catholic in his thinking and for this reason the breach with Rome was not immediate. In fact, Henry probably did not intend there to be a breach at all. He almost certainly assumed that the annulment would be granted. However, the Pope was not convinced of Henry's case and the King became increasingly angry. In 1531 he publicly separated from Queen Catherine of Aragon but still received no communication from the Pope that his annulment would be granted. Thus, in January 1533 the King went through a form of marriage privately with Anne Boleyn. This marriage was solemnised publicly in April of the same year and in June Archbishop Cramner granted the annulment independently of Rome. Pope Clement VII promptly declared the second union of Henry invalid and on 23 March 1534 he declared the first marriage to Catherine of Aragon the valid one. Traditionally only Rome could grant annulments and therefore Cramner's granting of an annulment had made the split from Rome definitive. It remained only for the Act of Succession to be passed declaring the king and his successors Head of the English Church. This momentous event occurred in June 1534. Unfortunately, however, King Henry's new marriage to Anne Boleyn did not last and he went on to contract four more marriages. Had the union between Henry and Anne lasted one might have legitimately considered that the judgement of the Church had been cruel and harsh and that the marriage to Catherine had been invalid and that the annulment should have been granted. However, as King Henry VIII went on to murder his second wife Anne Boleyn and also to marry, use and abuse a further four women his example was that of a sexist despot. Pope Clement VII, in comparison, seems to have been a discerning Pope who was able to see through the selfish whims of this King early on. He took the side of the King's first wife Queen Catherine of Aragon and discerned her to be a holy woman and indeed she went on to live a holy and blameless life.

Once the breach with Rome had taken place Henry was obviously free to do as he wished with the English Church. He could, of course, have merely taken over the monasteries and allowed them to continue. This is clearly what the last Abbess of Syon, Agnes Jordan, had expected him to do because the nuns of Syon who reluctantly accepted the King's new title (unlike some priests and deacons of Syon who resisted more passionately and strongly) immediately sent a message to Cromwell stating that they hoped he should 'be a good maister unto thaim and to thaire house, as thaire special trust is in you'. However, King Henry clearly had no intention to allow the monasteries to survive and the last Abbess of Syon was sadly naïve to expect the same. He had immediately begun a campaign to suppress the monasteries following the Act of Succession of 1533. Trevelyan states this policy was probably decided because the King's wars in France had emptied his treasuries and he was bankrupt. The monasteries were an obvious source of wealth and for this political reason the King seized them in stages and sold most of his monastic land. However, it is startling to note that despite all the mainstream cultural milieu of the day i.e., poems, songs etc which seemed to indicate that the nun wore her veil unwillingly - apparently only a very small proportion of nuns agreed or desired to be released from their vows. Despite evidence of some bad practice the majority of religious women in England appeared to want to spend the rest of their lives in the nunneries where they had originally taken their vows.

The extinction of the nunneries in England was a slow and insidious process. Following the Act of Succession, the King could select houses to stay in being. He allowed 43 nunneries to continue but this was a temporary measure. There were also some unofficial exemptions. However, those given respite were forced out by Cromwell. It was ensured that they had a lack of independence and a lack of freedom of manoeuvre. In addition, they were bullied and cajoled. During the final phase of liquidation Dr. John London was famous for his lack of sensitivity. Of him the Abbess of Bulkeley wrote:

'He here doth threaten me and my susters; saying that he hathe the Kynges commyssyon to suppres the house spite of my tethe. And when I ...shewyd him playne that I wolde never surrender to his hande, beying my awyncyent enemye, now he begynes to intreate me and to inveigle my susters one by one otherwise than ever I harde tell that any of the Kynges subjects hathe been handelyd.'

No- one, not even in our current secular age, can fail to feel some sympathy for this abbess as she was clearly bullied and cajoled until she was forced to give up a lifestyle that she loved. This abbess was eventually pensioned off just like the Abbess of Syon Agnes Jordan. It was simply not possible for women to withstand the power of King Henry and his new state. Persuasion, manipulation and the hard logic of the changing times brought the most die-hard religious woman to capitulate as there were no other alternatives open to her.

Those who did not wish to surrender could only flee and that is what happened to many of the Brigettines of Syon. Others remained and appeared to live ordinary lives but, although secularised, many of these women still considered themselves bound by their vows and never married.

Once the monasteries had been dissolved all their wealth was transferred to the King. Plate and silver were sent to the royal treasury and the furniture and domestic stuff was auctioned. Lead, woodwork, benches, grates, locks and other things were sold on the spot or sent to London. The churches were pulled down as were the steeples, cloisters and chapter houses. Sometimes as a cheaper option the buildings were defaced. A significant part of English heritage disappeared and with this the female consecrated life of the day.

While the disappearance of the female consecrated life at the time of the reformation can be noted and observed in the disappearance of the monasteries, we should also be aware of the disappearance of the vowesses who were still fairly numerous at the time of the reformation. As has been noted these vowesses were consecrated widows who lived independently but who might perhaps choose to live near a monastery or convent. There remained a significant number of them at the time of the reformation and some, although not all, were associated in a loose way with the monastery of Syon. Wood (2017) states that the religious profession of these widows was halted alongside the dissolution of the monasteries and that they gradually died off in the 1540's. They were never seen again in Britain until recent times when a few of them have re-emerged despite the lack of a universal rite of consecration.

On the death of Henry VIII his young son Edward (from Jane Seymour) came to the throne but this reign was to be short-lived. During the brief reign of King Edward VI, who was crowned at the age of nine, the mood of the times was really a continuation of the mood that had prevailed during the time of his father. During Edward's reign the realm was governed by a Regency Council because he had not and would never reach his age of majority as he died at 15 years of age. The council was first led by his uncle Edward Seymour and later by John Dudley. Under these relatives of his the reformation continued unabated as they were extremely pro-reform and the young Edward was manipulated by them being too young to have any definitive opinions himself. However, none of these could see any value in the female religious life or indeed in any Christian ministry for women in the church. Consecrated women simply ceased to exist as they had either been pensioned off on condition that they did not promote their way of life or they had fled in order to remain as religious in exile.

After the death of Edward, which was a short five years after he ascended to the throne, he was followed by his half-sister, Mary Tudor, who was Henry's Catholic daughter. Mary attempted to restore the religious life in England and the Brigettines of the Order of Syon, who had crossed the channel to escape the reformation, returned once again and made a brief attempt at re-establishment. The Dominican nuns were also rehoused. However, this revival was extremely short-lived. Mary reigned for only five years and on her death was succeeded by her protestant half-sister Elizabeth. When Elizabeth ascended to the throne these female religious women were again forced to flee and the sanctification of the clerical state to the exclusion of the religious again began unabated. Sadly, the reformation gave no real role or ministry to women at all other than being a 'holy wife' married to a priest or a religious man. The reformation was, in fact, very demeaning to women. No options were left open to them outside of marriage.

In 1603 the persecution of religious women in England could be seen in post reformation English canon law which dealt with the clerical and lay states and totally ignored the female consecrated state which had ceased to exist. To be consecrated in 1603 was not only not politically correct, it also placed one's life in danger. However, despite this the consecrated religious life was not to totally die out in England. It was to continue despite the reformation and its consequences. This continuation was to be brought about by one very remarkable woman and it was this woman and this woman alone who was to keep the flame of the consecrated life burning when all other religious hopes had been extinguished. Her name was Mary Ward.

Mary Ward was a woman who despite the mores of her time was determined to follow her inclination to tread the consecrated path. She was also a very original and deep-thinking woman and her thinking was to later lead to a new form of consecrated life not only in the English Catholic Church but also across the world. Mary was to offer Catholic women a new path and a new way. This way was the way of the active form of consecrated life. This way of life may, perhaps, have existed before with the hospitals of the early Middle Ages but had been a fleeting phenomenon. Mary was to make the active consecrated religious life definitive and universal and it was ironic that such a move should come from a woman who was of a nation that had almost totally abandoned the female religious life.

Mary Ward was born in 1586 of a well off northern recusant Catholic family and apparently two of her relatives were involved in the gunpowder plot. In 1595 her family home was burned down in an anti-Catholic riot and the children were saved by their father. She later developed the desire to live a celibate life and enter a religious order. However, there were no religious orders left in England and so Mary took the only option open to her and fled England for the low countries. Mary was not the only religious woman who took such action and the historian and nun Mary Paul (1936) stated that there was a long procession of English women who fled England in order to continue with their vocations. For these women the high romance of the religious vocation was made more glorious by the perils of answering its call. All these women were extraordinary but Mary was even more brave and extraordinary than these because she was eventually to return to England to live out her vocation.

In 1606 Mary entered a Belgium convent of the Poor Clares but she found that the contemplative life was not for her. She again tried her vocation at a second Poor Clare convent but this also did not work out and she eventually returned to England in 1609.

It was after her return to England that Mary developed the idea of an active religious order (later to be known as an institute or congregation) for women which, like the Jesuit Order for men, would teach and perform charitable works. Mary wanted a group of non-cloistered nuns without any distinctive habit who would be bound together by a rule and by a superior general. She managed to obtain the consent of Bishop Blaise of St Omer and in 1615 opened a branch of what was to be later known as the Institute. Steele (1901) states that the first convent was probably in St. Martin's Lane, London. Mary sent to Paul VI the scheme of the Institute and received a favourable reply. She founded a second convent at Fountains Abbey which was later moved to Heworth and then to the Bar, York. Mary's first convent also later moved to Hammersmith and for 120 years these two convents founded by Mary were the only communities of nuns in the whole of the country. This is remarkable in itself because it takes an extraordinary person of sure conviction to stand totally alone against the tide. Mary lived at a time when the consecrated life in England had been totally obliterated and wiped out. The nation saw no value in such a lifestyle and Mary was completely alone. There was no one, other than the few women gathered around her, with whom Mary could sympathise. And yet Mary kept the candle of the consecrated life burning with her two single convents in a land that wanted none of the same. She was a woman of trust but her trust was not in the society around her. Her trust was in the God she believed guided her. This then was the secret of Mary Ward. She was a woman driven by a force and this force enabled her to defy the mood of the times around her and even risk death. This force Mary knew as the Christian God.

While Mary was a woman of vision, she attracted like-minded women around her. All the early sisters of her congregation were extraordinary as they suffered great persecution in England. On occasions they were imprisoned and on another occasion the Bar convent was in danger of being destroyed by a fanatical mob. It was quite a miracle that this congregation survived and from the ashes of the reformation there would eventually come a new spring.

The persecution of the new congregation in England was not the only hardship that Mary and her sisters faced. The tide was also against them overseas. In 1629 the Congregation of the Propaganda suppressed Mary's Institute and stated that religious women should be enclosed and not active. Mary herself was imprisoned for a time in the Anger convent at Munich but eventually she managed to obtain the permission required for some of her sisters to continue their apostolate in England. However, this was only under the condition that they lived private vows. Mary's new congregation did not receive official recognition until its rule was eventually approved by Clement XI. The Institute itself was not given formal approval until 1877 which was 232 years after Mary's death. By this time many new congregations were springing up around the world. All of them based their rule on Mary's original ideal of the active religious life. Thus, it was Mary, a recusant single minded English woman living in hostile times, who changed the worldwide face of the female ministry in the universal Catholic Church.

Mary had given the female consecrated life a resurrection. Prior to Mary's congregation religious women who wished, since the time of the reformation, to live a celibate life in community were meant to be fully enclosed. Post reformation women prior to Mary lived lives which were dominated by the offices of Prime, Tierce, Sext, None, Vespers, Compline and Night. The duty of these nuns was to say these offices and spend the rest of their life in prayer in an enclosed convent. Mary's new congregation of consecrated women were not nuns. They were sisters. The new sisters were women who combined a reformed life of prayer with an active life. Some would term them contemplatives in action. These sisters and all the new congregations that would emulate them would be fully involved in teaching, nursing and many other professions across the world. However, the enclosed form of consecrated life did not die out and to this day there remain two forms of religious life. There are those who live an enclosed and prayerful contemplative life and those who live an unenclosed and active life rooted in prayer. The first group of women are known as nuns. The second group of women are not, strictly speaking, nuns. They may be sisters or they may be following some of the other forms of consecrated life that have been recently restored or some of the new forms of consecrated life that have come into being since Vatican II. However, in common terms the name 'nun' is often applied to all women who currently follow a consecrated life. This term is canonically incorrect when used for all consecrated

women and should only be used for those women who are
fully enclosed.

Chapter Five

Active Religious Congregations (Modernists and Reformers)

'I hope in God that it will be seen that women in time to come will do much' –Mary Ward

The reformation and its after effects did nothing for women and their intellectual standing. It has already been noted how in the Anglo-Saxon church and also in the church of the early Middle Ages women were very influential. Women had wielded influence as matriarchs, anchorites and mystics but prior to the reformation their influence had declined due to the mores and values of the time. Even the great Syon which was a place of intellectual learning could not boast of one particular woman who was to have a major effect on society. Nor could it boast, at the time of the Reformation when martyrdom was rife, of any female martyrs. The martyrs who arose from its walls were men. With the arrival of the reformation the position of women in society became still worse. This was because prior to the reformation there had always been another alternative to marriage available to women – the consecrated life. Now, with the reformation and its after effects, this alternative was no longer available. A woman's only option was marriage. She was now literally confined to the service of a man and the domestic life.
The great Mary Ward, that early pioneer of the emancipation of women, was aware of the decline in women's status due to the reformation. In 1616 she stated:
'I hope in God that it will be seen that women in time to come will do much.'

However even the fruits of Mary's own labour were not to be seen for at least two hundred years and for the moment the spirit of the British woman was suppressed whatever her inclinations and aspirations. It would be celibate women who would begin the release of the spirit of the British Catholic woman but this phenomenon would not occur for nearly two hundred years. The post reformation period represented a dark age for all women regardless of birth, status, age or intellectual capabilities.

While the English state had albeit succeeded in ridding itself of the nunneries and other female celibate woman, meanwhile in the rest of Europe dark times were also dawning for any woman who had any form of inclination to live a style of consecrated life. With the arrival of the French revolution monasteries were dissolved in France, Belgium, Germany, Italy and Spain and it was thought that the consecrated life was done with forever. However, the persecution did not last and within a generation the restoration movement was in place. Pope Pius VII was eager to provide a model for restoring the orders.

The French revolution was important for Catholic women in England because it was during the course of that revolution that religious women once again returned to English shores. Celibate women who had fled England in search of a place to live out their vows overseas now fled continental Europe for England in pursuit of the same mission. In England the times were changing and the country was again becoming more receptive to having religious women in its midst.

In 1792 the Benedictine nuns of Montergis arrived in England and a home was found for them. These nuns were treated like heroines and the fact that they belonged to a church that was still regarded with deep suspicion was forgotten. The Benedictines were allowed to expand and by 1794 they were at Winchester; Hammersmith; Marnhull and Preston. In addition to the Benedictines other religious women of other orders began to arrive and establish themselves. These were the Canonesses of St. Augustine at Suffolk; the Canonesses of the Holy Sepulchre at Holme Hall and the Carmelites at Lanherne, Bishop Auckland and Acton. The Dominicans also re-established themselves at Gloucester and the Poor Clares arrived in Northumberland. A new age was dawning in England for the female religious life. The religious woman had reappeared and convents were once again built in England. By 1825 the people of England were once again used to having religious women in their midst.

After the French revolution the female religious life began once again to flourish in Europe and it was at this stage that Mary Ward's idea of the active religious life began to take root. Many new active congregations began to spring up across the continent. In the main these congregations were devoted to carrying out works of charity and also to providing a Catholic education for the young. The women who joined them were very different to the women who lived the enclosed life. The enclosed life demands a very special charism from a woman who is able and willing to retire from the world and live, either alone or in a religious community, a life of prayer and contemplation. However, these women were independent spirits who desired to live active and innovative lives in the world as bearers of reform. They raised monies to build schools and hospitals and they began to bring about great changes in English society. Like their enclosed counterparts they were driven with a desire to unite with and serve God but their way was achieved through bringing about social justice in the world around them rather than through living a life of contemplative prayer. The church now considered both ways acceptable. The lives of these active women were however in the spirit of the times and they considered themselves to be contemplatives in action. Their lives were rooted in prayer but they also played an active part in the world. By this time the rules of enclosure were modified and due to this the number of vocations increased everywhere. There were numerous women who felt called to live the religious life in its new active form and there was plenty of work, in the realms of social justice, to be done.

Within England both religious congregations from the continent and new home-grown congregations were to take root. England, of course, remained a protestant country and the number of women putting themselves forward for the religious life could never equal numbers like those in France. However, even so, the growth in the number of convents in England was phenomenal. By 1929 there were 892 Catholic convents in England and Wales. While this did not compare with the 16,298 convents in France by 1890, it was a long way from the two convents which had existed in England during the times of Mary Ward.

The new religious women who dedicated themselves to active causes within England had a remarkable effect on English society. This effect was at first to be felt in Catholic circles because these women were Catholic. However partly as a result of the presence of these active Catholic religious women in England the Anglican Church as well was to see a new resurgence in its female religious life and some Anglican women also decided to take the path of consecrated life. The Anglican religious life was revived in the mid-nineteenth century with the Oxford Movement and during this period both contemplative and active religious orders were founded within the Anglican Church.

Within the Catholic Church the sphere in which the active religious woman was to have the most effect was the sphere of education. In this field female active religious women were to have a far greater effect in England than they did on the continent. There was a great determination emanating from religious communities to build schools for the Catholic community and they made available an education for girls which had not previously existed except perhaps in Anglo Saxon England. However, in Anglo Saxon England an excellent female education had only been available to the aristocracy. These women provided an education for girls which was available to a much broader section of the community. By 1850 mainstream England still offered few opportunities for women apart from marriage but within the Catholic community a quiet revolution was taking place. Mainstream England at this time had no public schools for girls and its universities were closed to the female sex but the Catholic community boasted a formidable number of convent schools. These schools concentrated on providing an education for girls which equalled that of boys.

The new religious women who founded and taught at convent schools across the nation did not see teaching as simply a job. For these women teaching was a sacred calling.

It was a vocation and their whole lives were dedicated to serving God through this medium. Of these women was demanded an extraordinary sacrifice far beyond that of working the long hours of 9am to 8pm that many teachers sometimes do today. Many of the schools concerned were boarding schools and required a round the clock working day and due to the fact that the women lived in community, they were expected to cover. There was no help from outside because in those days the women felt they had to do everything themselves. The service of the children was regarded as paramount and the sisters were expected to put the children above themselves and their own desires. Some congregations, such as La Sainte Union, even had to take a fourth simple vow emphasising the fact that they would do everything for the well-being of the children in their care even to the point of death and the sacrifice of their own lives. Today it has become very fashionable to denigrate these women and it is true that on some occasions children were physically punished by a minority of the sisters in religious orders of the time. However, during that era corporal punishment was the cultural norm of the time and the sisters, if they did apply it, were acting in accordance with what their current society believed to be the best practice. 'Spare the rod, spoil the child', was regarded as a common cultural practice across mainstream Britain. It would therefore be unfair in current times to judge and write off these women due to the fact they did not live according to the cultural norms of our day. Our cultural norms follow advances in psychology that these women living in that particular era knew nothing about. The majority of these women did their best in their time to elevate the education of girls in their society. They were actually great reformers and were in front of the thinking of their times rather than behind.

While female education was taking great strides forward within the Catholic community in England this was still not reflected in the nation as a whole. In 1868 the School's Enquiry Commission emphasised the poor quality of female education. By this time there were over twenty different congregations of religious sisters engaged in teaching and they offered an imposing selection of convent schools for the Catholic girl which were the envy of mainstream England. Some of these schools were by now schools of longstanding such as the Bar Convent at York which had been founded by Mary Ward herself.

The female religious women of the nineteenth century had made great strides in the sphere of female education at primary and secondary level but their influence was not to stop there. After the schools had been established female religious began also to establish teacher training colleges through their own fundraising and at their own expense. While the Church in 1850 was funding and establishing a teacher's training college for men the female religious women received no such help. They founded their own colleges independently. It may have been the case that even the institution of the Catholic Church in England could not keep up with its female celibate women and may not have fully appreciated the strides they were making. These women were exceptional in their day and in order to fully appreciate this it is necessary to take a closer look at the religious congregations active in England at this time.

One of the first congregations to arrive in England were the Sisters of Mercy. They came from Ireland in 1839 and within a week they had six English postulants. The Sisters of Mercy had been founded in 1827 by Catherine McAulay. Catherine was of a distinguished Irish family who all converted to Protestantism at a time when the idea of the 'Church Triumphant' was prominent in all denominations. Nothing would induce Catherine to change her Catholic religion which was quite a feat when all her family had done the same. Catherine inherited a large fortune and wanted to put this to the service of the Catholic Church and the poor. She was a very determined and strong-minded woman of vision. She founded a congregation that was dedicated to both serving the sick and aiding and educating the poor. Steele (1901) stated that the education of the poor was close to Catherine's heart. As a result of this wherever a Convent of Mercy was found in England there was also a school. Catherine's congregation was also concerned with providing a Catholic education for the middle classes. Catherine saw general education and religious education as closely tied together and believed that a good education could not be provided without the moral basis which religion also gives. Shortly after the arrival of the Sisters of Mercy in 1839 the Sacred Heart sisters arrived in 1842. They had been founded by Sister Madeleine Sophie Barat in 1800 and aimed to dedicate their lives to the work of education in secondary boarding schools; day schools; elementary schools and orphanages. They based the education they gave on the study of religion and philosophy and, like the Sisters of Mercy, could not envisage how it was possible to deliver an excellent education without the moral grounding that finds its base in religion. The Society of the Sacred Heart became one of the leading Institutes of Catholic education in England and built a large number of schools.

After the arrival of the Sacred Heart sisters the expansion of the female Catholic teaching congregations continued unabated and in 1843 the Institute of Charity arrived at Loughborough. Shortly afterwards they were followed by the Notre Dame sisters at Penryn and the Sisters of the Holy Child Jesus. In 1850 Cardinal Wiseman took over the guidance of the English Catholic Church and he invited many more of the new congregations to England. This resulted in still more schools for girls being established. There were also 'home-grown' English congregations which were founded here and which established and developed schools. The Sisters of the Holy Cross and Passion were founded in Manchester in 1851 for educational purposes and also for the sick and under privileged. These sisters were founded by Fr. Ignatius Spencer an ancestor of the late Diana Princess of Wales. Within a few years they had established schools at Bolton, Salford, Sutton, Dewsbury and Huddersfield.

Among the congregations invited to England by Cardinal Wiseman were the Congregation of the Holy Union of the Sacred Hearts of Jesus and Mary (La Sainte Union) which arrived in 1859 and the Sisters of Charity of St. Vincent de Paul which arrived at about the same time. La Sainte Union was to become one of the most important congregations in educational work. By 1901 it had seven schools of importance in England and in 1904 it opened a teacher's training college which would later become part of the University of Southampton. These sisters saw teaching as a vocation in itself and, as has already been noted, had to take a fourth simple vow which emphasised the fact that they would sacrifice their own lives, if required, for the sake of the children in their care. With Catholic teaching dominated by congregations such as these the standing and esteem of the teacher was elevated to a very high level indeed.

While La Sainte Union made pioneering attempts to provide the average Catholic family with a good education for its children, the Sisters of Charity of St. Vincent de Paul specialised in helping those with special needs and were pioneers in another sphere, that of informing society of the value of all human beings regardless of disability. These sisters opened schools for deaf; speechless and blind children in addition to also opening schools for children with learning disabilities and for orphans.

By 1860 the British Catholic woman was well ahead of her time in England not only in providing an education for girls at a time when the nation still regarded its women as fodder for marriage but also through the vision of providing an education for those with all sorts of disabilities including learning difficulties. It was to be at least another hundred years before the nation was ever to fully tackle the problem of educating people with disabilities and when it did it so it would be because this path had already been indicated by Catholic religious women. British society may have forgotten the contribution that these women made and it is a good time to be reminded of the same. Catholic religious women led the way in the emancipation of those disregarded by society, namely their own sex and also the disabled and disadvantaged. Catholic religious women could also be regarded as the first career women in modern Britain. While the majority of English women were tied to domestic duties and the service of a man the British Catholic religious women were running schools and hospitals and had a great sphere of influence both within the Church and the nation.

After 1860 the growth of religious congregations under Cardinal Manning continued. The Daughters of the Cross of Liege arrived and established themselves at Cheltenham; Chelsea; Bury and Manchester. They were swiftly followed by the Sisters of the Sacred Heart of Mary who desired to educate all classes of society and established boarding schools and day schools for the middle classes as well as poor schools, industrial schools, night schools and orphanages for the disadvantaged. It would not be and is not appropriate for us today, living as we do in a different and later society with different cultural and societal norms, to criticise the fact that these sisters chose to educate the middle classes separately to those children who were poorer. These sisters lived in a different era with different social norms and during the time in which they lived they were actually pioneers. They had an inclusive view of society which involved educating all humanity regardless of class status. They were in front of their times and in their view, a better society could only come about if all people rich or poor, understood the love of God.

Numerous other congregations followed the congregations above in involving themselves in the education of the Catholic community. Some of these congregations were the Sisters of St. Joseph of Peace who established themselves at Nottingham, Leicester and Grimsby and the Religious of the Cross who established schools at Boscombe, Waterlooville and the Isle of Wight. In 1880 La Retraite arrived in England and they established schools at Clapham Park, Burnham, Clifton and Weston-Super-Mare. This congregation was swiftly followed by the Dames of Christian Instruction (1891) who established schools at Dorset and Surrey and the Sisters of the Christian Schools of Mercy who arrived in 1894. The original founding congregation of the Institute of the Blessed Virgin Mary also began to establish new schools in England at Ascot, Gloucester and Cambridge.

By 1900 the female religious movement was a force to be reckoned with in England and it had made remarkable achievements and strides in Catholic minority England in the sphere of education. Catholic girls now basked in being the recipients of the best ever education for girls offered in England for over a thousand years. The rest of the country had, however, began to notice these strides and was attempting to catch up. In 1869 the Endowed Schools Act encouraged the erection of girls' schools. University colleges for girls, such as Lady Margaret Hall and Somerville, also began to be established. This meant that the Catholic religious woman had not only been an influence in society within Catholic circles – she had also been a pioneering example to the nation as a whole. Her rise in the last half of the nineteenth century and also the first half of the twentieth century was phenomenal and nothing, at the time, could prevent the ascension of her star. New religious congregations continued to arrive in England throughout this period and in 1902 the Missionary Sisters of the Sacred Heart established a school as did the Sisters of St. Martin of Tours in 1904.

While female religious women in England had found and developed their own careers through taking the celibate path, they were also anxious to ensure that women who did not wish to become nuns or sisters should also be able to pursue their own careers. For this reason, female celibate women were instrumental in establishing teacher training colleges which would enable women to become teachers without becoming religious sisters. In 1901 La Sainte Union opened a teacher's training college at Southampton and by 1950 there were 11 such teacher training colleges in England which had been established by different religious congregations. For this reason, the modern lay teacher of today is indebted to the modern and reforming celibate woman of yesterday.

The English religious women's pioneering foundation of teacher training colleges which were to produce lay teachers was also to eventually result in their own withdrawal from the educational sphere. This was because as the state began to follow their example and to take over education in the twentieth century on the lines they had proposed - it also began to squeeze them out and as the number of lay teachers increased the number of religious teachers began to decline.

It was during the period of 1920 – 1950 that the number of religious women engaged in education was to reach its pinnacle. By 1920 the Catholic community had a range of boarding schools far beyond any other section of English society. There were also at this time in England more convent schools than anywhere else in the world. These schools, many of which were for girls only, caused the number of schools for girls within the Catholic community to outnumber the number of schools for boys by 5 to 1. This fact is little known and remembered and illustrates the difference in opportunity available to the Catholic, as opposed to the non-Catholic English girl. At this time there were not many independent schools for non-Catholic girls in existence in England but by 1948 there were 336 schools in the Association of Convent Schools and these belonged to over a hundred distinct congregations. These schools were held in high esteem outside the Catholic community and many non-Catholics began to send their children there. Eventually they became the envy not only of non-Catholic England but also of Europe.

The Convent schools which had been built in England by the various religious congregations were eventually to be replaced by lay Catholic schools. Some of these schools were very good but it has been argued that overall, they never quite matched the excellence of the independent Catholic schools. One of the problems that has faced the English Catholic Church since the closure of most of its convent schools has been that of locality. The convent schools were small and were found eventually in almost every small town. However, the state could not fund such small schools and the lay schools that followed them were built in areas that would serve three or perhaps four small towns. The result was that Catholic children had to travel to receive an education and some parents were not willing to send their children to school on a bus. This led to a decline in the take-up of Catholic education with some Catholic parents electing on a non-Catholic education for their children. The new state Catholic schools also did not have the same freedom with the curriculum that the independent Catholic schools had enjoyed.

This chapter has thus far concentrated on the work of the religious women in the sphere of education and it has been noted that within this area great strides were made by these women. Not only did they supply girls with an excellent education, they were also pivotal in bringing about the social reforms that led to the creation of a state education for all. However, the pioneering religious women of the time did not only bring about reforms in the field of education. They were influential in other spheres as well; the main one being that of social work.

In 1846 Cornelia Conelly, an American woman who had been married but had together with her husband given up the married state to become a religious, came to England. She founded the Society of the Holy Child and her first convent was at Derby. While this society too was dedicated to education and opened various schools, it was also devoted to works of charity. It had a spirituality of simplicity, obedience and love which Anson described as been expressed by the dictum of 'Action – not Words'. The foundress's wish was that her congregation would meet the needs of the age by serving those who were disadvantaged.

In 1853 another purely English congregation devoted to works of charity was founded by Margaret Hallahan and this was a congregation of Dominican sisters who were dedicated to emulating the spirit of St Catherine of Siena. Again, this congregation was active in education but it was also active in the sphere of charity and caring for the disadvantaged. Some of the schools that were founded were devoted purely to the care of those with severe disabilities or learning disabilities and they provided a quality of life for disabled children that was not as yet known in England. At the time there were no state schools for children with learning disabilities and once again religious women were pioneers breaking new ground in the social care field. The sisters combined social action with the contemplative life and had a rich prayer life which involved praying for the spiritual sanctification of all humanity as well as adoration of the Blessed Sacrament. The final purely English congregation to be mentioned here is one which was founded by Fanny Margaret Taylor in 1870. This congregation was known as The Poor Servants of the Mother of God. Fanny Margaret Taylor had been a nurse under Florence Nightingale in the Crimea and had later become a Catholic. She opened her first convent in Mount St London in 1868. The aim of her sisters was to work among the poor. The constitution of her congregation was eventually approved in 1885. The apostolate of the sisters consisted in nursing the sick; hospital care; providing refuge for those who were outcast from society and other charitable works. They also attempted to care for the mentally ill who were a group much neglected in England at the time.

In Britain (and particularly in England) during the period of 1792 to 1950 the Catholic Church expanded rapidly and made great strides in the sphere of education and social work which were eventually to lead the whole nation towards establishing better education and social care. Most of these strides were made by celibate women who led the way not only in the emancipation of all women but also in the emancipation of the nation. The English state was to emulate its celibate women in providing the opportunities they had created for the Catholic community for the whole nation. However, the contribution that these women made to English society has never been fully recognised by the state and, it could be argued, by the Catholic Church itself.

Chapter Six

Post Vatican II decline and beginnings of 21st century renewal

The previous chapter illustrated how active consecrated women transformed education for girls in England and gave them opportunities not available to the majority of girls in British society. These opportunities were sought after and eventually emulated by the rest of the nation. The contribution of these women had thus had a very direct effect on the establishment of state education. The religious women had been reformers and evangelisers and through their influence in schools in particular had caused the Catholic Church in England to grow rapidly. However, humanity is always in transition and the influence of the active consecrated women of the nineteenth and early twentieth centuries would not last. This chapter will look at the decline of the active consecrated religious life in England within the Catholic Church in the late twentieth century; the message of Vatican II and the changes to the female consecrated life which it brought about; the initial post conciliar decline of the female consecrated life in Britain following Vatican II and the current beginnings of a small new revival of consecrated life in a variety of forms in the twenty first century.

By 1950, 43 percent of all those who attended Catholic schools were non-Catholic and naturally as a result of this the number of Catholics in England had increased. This was because many of the non-Catholics who attended these schools later went on to convert to the Catholic faith.

However, by now it could be argued that the Catholic Church was becoming more inward looking and this inward-looking approach would be one of the factors which would lead to its decline in Britain in the late twentieth century.

The spirit of the new age could be seen in the writings of the Rev. Battersley (1950) who lamented the fact that most convent schools took in a large number of non-Catholics. His was not an evangelical or inclusive approach. By 1950 there were 27,000 Catholic girls who were educated in convent schools as well as several thousand boys. However over 20,000 non-Catholic girls were also receiving a convent school education. The entire system of Catholic education was in the hands of female religious women and Battersley did write prophetically that without a continuation in the number of vocations the whole structure would collapse. But one wonders how vocations were to increase if the church was going to cease to be evangelical as he also lamented the fact that many non-Catholics were receiving a Catholic education because they could afford to pay while many Catholics were denied the same. While his desire to see poor Catholics receive a good education was inclusive, his desire to exclude non-Catholics was neither inclusive nor evangelical. In the meantime, the Catholic Church had supported the 1944 Education Act which would lead to many of the convent schools eventually becoming state schools but would expect the female religious congregations to find the monies needed to bring their buildings up to the required standard. This was due to the fact that while the quality of teaching remained outstanding in these schools many of their buildings were becoming outdated compared to the new schools that were now being built everywhere by the state.

Meantime, while Catholic education was a topical subject to be debated hotly in Catholic circles around the country, the Catholic Church continued to grow for the moment at least. All other churches had declined in England during the period of 1900 – 1950 but the Catholic Church had continued to grow steadily after 1920 and would continue to do so until the late 1960's. To fail to recognise the role of the British religious women in this growth would be a fallacy. The schools that these women had created were attracting large numbers of non-Catholics and many of these non-Catholic girls did at a later date convert to the Catholic faith as a result of the witness of the selflessness they had seen epitomised in some of the women who were their teachers. Up until the late 1960s there was a steady growth in the number of priests, churches, schools and convents and one of the main factors behind this growth had been active British religious women. By 1961, 12.7 percent of all marriages were Catholic and 10 percent of the nation was practising Catholic. This was a remarkable feat considering that the Catholic Church had ceased to exist at all in this country post Reformation. Also, in 1961 a survey of church attendance in four Liverpool dioceses gave Catholics 81.6%, Anglicans 10.8% and Non-Conformists 4.2%. Catholic infant baptisms represented 15% of the nation's total live births and there were over 12,000 converts to the Catholic faith a year. Many of these converts discovered their faith through the example of love that had been shown to them by many of the active religious women who had educated them. This was a feat which has never properly been recognised by the British Catholic Church and certainly in more modern times the media has concentrated only on reporting the abuse which was experienced by a very small minority in these schools.

During the first half of the twentieth century when Catholicism was at its height in Britain, the spirituality of Catholicism was very different to the spirituality of the nation. The spirituality of the nation was, for non-Catholics, centred on Sunday worship at church, Sunday school classes and Bible school classes but the spirituality of the Catholic minority was very different to this. There was a Latin Mass which, while not understandable to the majority in the form of language, appeared in its 'mystique' to evoke a sense of the supernatural. The Bible was not widely read in Catholic circles because the focus was on personal spiritual experience through a mystical path to God rather than spirituality through reading the biblical books. Catholic spirituality appeared mystical and it involved seeking out the Absolute through mystical experiences such as focussing on the sufferings of humanity through remembering the sufferings of Christ. This remembering of Christ's sufferings could be seen in the cult of devotion to the Sacred Heart which represented the piercing of the Heart of the Sacred Jesus due to His Divine Love. Catholic spirituality in this regard was trying to be extremely profound by illustrating to everyone that suffering was normal in this life and part of being human. It would be experienced by every person in this world because all love can be seen as a wound which will eventually lead to pain. All temporal love will eventually lead to pain because the object of love will be lost either through death or other means. Catholic spirituality was therefore attempting to convey that the only love that is enduring is the love of God and through this love of God the individual could eventually be reconciled with his/her fellow human beings who had been lost through the effects of time. It could be argued that while Catholic spirituality concentrated on these mystical sufferings and experiences of all humanity Catholicism thrived. This is because after Vatican II there appeared to be in England, in the early years after the Council, a definite attempt to emulate the biblical focus of the Anglican Church and to take this on board and this did not always work. There is an argument which states that once Catholic spirituality ceased to be mystical and sought to emulate the biblical focus of the Anglican Church the decline of the Catholic Church in England in the late twentieth century began. However not all Anglicanism had a biblical focus. There were also Anglican religious orders in Britain which, while never as numerous as the Catholic religious orders, may not have experienced the decline in recent years that the Catholic religious orders have. These Anglican religious orders were generally regarded as 'high church'.

In 1962 when the Second Vatican Council met the picture was looking very rosy for the Catholic Church in Britain. There had not been, since prior to the reformation, as many Catholic Churches built or as many vocations. The effect of the Second Vatican Council was to initially change all this but it can be argued that this effect was never intended by the Council and was a result of the British Catholic Church's misinterpretation of the new teaching and other factors. Certainly, the countries that were Catholic, rather than

Protestant, at the time of Vatican II were not hit with such a decline in numbers and vocations as Britain was and this may have been because Britain interpreted the Second Vatican Council in a much more 'Protestant' (as in low rather than high church) way.

The Second Vatican Council was opened on 11 October 1962 by Pope St. John XXIII and closed under Pope St. Paul VI on the Feast of the Immaculate Conception on 8 December 1965. It was the twenty first ecumenical council of the Catholic Church and the second to be held at St. Peter's Basilica in the Vatican. The Council addressed relationships between the Catholic Church and the modern world. It also sought to renew the consecrated life; make ecumenical efforts towards dialogue with other religions and call everyone to holiness including the laity. Other changes which followed the Council included the widespread use of vernacular languages in the Mass instead of Latin; the revision of Eucharistic prayers; the abbreviation of the liturgical calendar; the ability to celebrate the Mass with the priest facing the congregation and modern aesthetic changes encompassing contemporary Catholic liturgical music and artwork.

Prior to the Second Vatican Council it could be argued that the church of the early twentieth century had been dominated by clergy and consecrated women and that the laity had assumed a passive role. Lay people had the sacraments given to them and they carried out acts of devotion such as novenas to the Sacred Heart but all the real ministries in the church were carried out by priests and consecrated women. Priests administered the sacraments and consecrated women taught in schools and worked in the sphere of social care. Vatican II sought to change this by defining the laity as the people of God who shared in the one priesthood of Christ which was grounded in the sacraments of baptism and confirmation. As a result of this there was in post conciliar times a great increase in lay ministries including the canonical ministries of reader and acolyte and also the ministries of teaching, music, social action and the distribution of the Blessed Sacrament.

In addition to increasing the number of ministries open to the laity and redefining the lay state Vatican II also laid down the foundations for a new theology of marriage which would put the married state on equal footing with the consecrated life. Prior to Vatican II the consecrated life had been seen as superior by the majority of the nation's Catholics but now Vatican II in its conciliar and post conciliar documents spoke of the lofty status of the marriage vocation and the sacredness of the bond. The sexual act was now seen as self-giving, holy and noble and bodily union was now a beautiful and dignified thing. This contrasted greatly with much earlier theology such as that of Augustine which had portrayed the union of the flesh as at best a remedy for the body's inclination to sin.

It took some time for the teachings of Vatican II to filter down to grass root level in Britain but when they did the result was initially a drastic falling off in the number of vocations to the female consecrated life. There was also a drastic falling off in the number of practicing lay Catholics.

The falling off in the number of practising lay Catholics in Britain may not entirely have been a result of Vatican II at all but partly a result of the effect of the state taking over education as this would have taken a while to filter through. However, it is also possible that the decline in the number of practicing lay Catholics could have been due to the fact that a certain proportion of the post conciliar laity thought too much was now expected of them. It takes a large commitment to bring up children well and many hardworking lay Catholics who were struggling to make ends meet and to bring up their children could, in the past, have sought advice, comfort and solace from a consecrated sister. However now this option seemed to be no longer available to them as the number of sisters was declining and the definite trend in Britain post Vatican II was suddenly for the laity to run the ministries in the church. In addition to that active female consecrated sisters in Britain seemed to interpret Vatican II as an indication that they should withdraw from their ministries and hand them over completely to the laity. This may have been a mistake because while many Catholic lay people welcomed the opportunity to take up the new lay ministries offered by Vatican II a significant number did not. This was not in any way because lay people could not carry out these ministries but because marriage is a vocation in itself and bringing up children is very hard work. Many married lay people had in the past enjoyed the counselling and support of active female consecrated women to assist them when they struggled with their own vocation but this was now being withdrawn from them. These lay people were also too busy working in their own spheres to take up lay ministries in the church and they lamented the loss of the full time female religious women who would support them in regards to their lay marital state within the world. They also still looked towards these sisters, who they saw as full-time ministers, to take the lead in setting up prayer and bible study groups but the sisters, unfortunately, no longer saw these as their remit alone and expected the lay people to set up the same.

There was also another thornier issue that may have driven lay Catholics from the church in the post Vatican II period and this was the Papal Encyclical 'Humanae Vitae' promulgated by Pope Paul VI. This encyclical affirmed traditional church moral teaching on the sanctity of life and the procreative and unitive nature of conjugal relations.
However, while the encyclical acknowledges that there are circumstances in which a married couple would desire to limit the size of their family it condemns artificial birth control and advocates instead natural birth control taking advantage of infertile cycles within the reproductive system. This had not been expected because the church post Vatican II had seemed to become much more positive in regards to sexuality and the document was received with shock. Open dissent from the laity was also voiced widely and publicly. There was also a group of dissident theologians led by Rev. Charles Curran which issued a statement that Catholics should decide about artificial contraception in accordance with their conscience. In Britain this teaching was widely rejected and was another factor that led to Catholics leaving the church. The majority of those that decided to remain also rejected the teaching almost universally and this can be evidenced at any Sunday Family Mass in current times. The

number of couples with more than two children are very few and far between.

In regards to this massive decline of the Catholic Church in Britain after the Second Vatican Council Hastings also postulates a variety of reasons. He states that the obvious and overwhelming differences between Catholic and other Christian theology had been removed by Vatican II. The Mass was now in English and Catholic translations of the Bible in English had been introduced. The previous mystical spirituality of the Catholic Church was on the wane and there was concentration on Bible study classes and the 'Word of God'. The lay state had been sanctified and lay people were much more involved in the running of the church. There was now little to differentiate the Catholic Church from other Protestant Churches and for this reason it lost its attraction. While there is obviously some truth in Hastings' claims it is likely that these are just some factors amongst many. Another factor that may have led to the decline of the British Catholic Church and in particular the decline of the female consecrated life after the Second Vatican Council was almost certainly the confusion that initially followed it. This confusion was partially generated by the sudden elevation of marriage to a holy state on an equal footing with celibacy. This does not mean that the Council was wrong to elevate marriage. In fact, this was a reform that was very necessary and long awaited but the sudden introduction of this reform led to a lot of questions. One question that was raised at the time was that if marriage was so holy why bother to be a priest or a consecrated woman? Another question was if marriage was so holy why should there not be a married priesthood? This of course is a question that continues to be asked by Catholics today.

As a result of this kind of confusion a leading figure in the Church, Fr. Charles Davis, suddenly announced he was leaving the priesthood. Charles Alfred Davis was an English theologian and priest and Professor of Theology at Heythrop College in the University of London. He had been educated at the Pontifical Gregorian University in Rome and had been ordained in 1946. He was the first Catholic to give the F.D. Maurice Lectures at Kings College London which were published in 1966 as 'God's Grace in History'. He was also the editor of a famous periodical of the time known as 'Clergy Review'. His announcement that he was leaving the priesthood was a major shock to the nation's Catholics and in particular its' priests and active consecrated sisters. From this point on other religious men and women began to abandon their vocations and the decline of the religious orders and congregations began once again in Britain. Fewer women began to offer themselves as sisters for the active consecrated life and many large convents closed. Consecrated sisters began to move into smaller houses. The nation's convent schools which had been the envy of Europe began to close on masse. Where as in the 1960s most Catholic schools were run by religious orders and had consecrated sisters as their head teachers, by the end of the 1970s there were far fewer Catholic schools in general and most of them had lay head teachers. These changes were not wrong, in fact it could be argued that they were welcome and it was desirable that the laity were more involved in the running of Catholic schools. The problem was more how there was in Britain, post Vatican II, a sudden extreme shift from the female consecrated sisters to the laity not only in the running of schools but in all ministries and this led to widespread confusion. In other European countries, such as Italy, the active religious sisters remained and were working alongside the laity in collaborative ministry.

Although there was widespread confusion in Britain about the role and place of both the consecrated sisters and the laity in society this had certainly not been the vision or intention of the Second Vatican Council. The Council had envisaged a new collaborative ministry in which the new lay ministers worked side by side with consecrated women. The Council produced numerous documents on the consecrated life such as the initial inclusion of the consecrated state in Lumen Gentium and the decrees on the renewal of the consecrated life and on contemplatives. All these decrees emphasised the Council's high regard for the female consecrated life but the sentiments expressed in these religious documents did not appear to filter down in Britain. In the UK no one appeared to see the value or worth of the consecrated life anymore and it was portrayed in an increasingly negative way. In particular Britain was now in the grips of a sexual revolution and the abstention from sex which is required of the consecrated woman was portrayed in a particularly derogative way by the modern media. This was because where-as once in Victorian England women had been expected to abstain from sexual relationships outside of marriage; in the late twentieth century sex was regarded as compulsory whatever one's marital status. Anyone who did not wish to follow this trend was regarded as 'odd' or 'repressed'. Britain had swung from one extreme to another.

In 1970 in the wake of the Second Vatican Council Pope St Paul VI reintroduced the rite of consecrated virgins living in the world. This rite was an ancient one which had died out with the founding of abbeys and convents from the sixth century onwards. The re-introduction of the rite initially had little impact on a Britain that was in the grip of a sexual revolution although it did have some impact in other European countries. In countries such as France and Italy there was a high take up of this vocation and this form of consecrated life quickly established itself alongside the religious congregations.

Vatican II had opened the doors of the church to lay people and enabled them to serve God in a variety of ministries but it could be argued that in the Britain of the late twentieth century the vision of Vatican II did not work out very well. This was because while the inclusion of the laity in the church's ministry was a welcome one and would lead to many talents being tapped which had previously laid dormant; a large number of lay people were not prepared to get involved with the church in the way the Council had envisaged. There were a significant number of lay people who welcomed the opportunity to become eucharistic ministers; readers; musicians; Sunday school teachers or members of the parish council but many other lay people did not want to be bothered. For them holding down a job and maintaining a marriage was hard enough in itself without taking on the running of their local church as well. Sitting on a parochial council or managing church finances simply did not appeal. The other problem was that many lay people who were married and in full time work still felt the need of support from religious sisters and the writer can recall hearing many such people lamenting their decline in numbers. However here in Britain the active consecrated women themselves now felt obliged to withdraw from their ministries to make way for the laity and began to take deliberate steps back and in effect signed their own death warrants. In addition to this, sermons began to be preached by priests week in and week out exhorting the laity to become involved with the main phrase usually being, 'Forget about priests and nuns; you are the church.' However, many lay people simply did not want to be involved in this way and this may have been one of the factors that led to a large number of them leaving the church. The problem seemed to be that within the church there had always been men and women that held full time ministries and took leadership roles in their communities. Now consecrated women were increasingly side-lined and becoming more and more part time. There were no longer full-time ministries for consecrated women in the church but the full-time ministry of priest remained and the British Church thus became increasingly clericalised. It could also be argued that the way Vatican II was being promoted in Britain was not, in fact, what the Council had intended. The Council had not intended active consecrated women to back out completely in order to make way for a prospective vast army of part time lay people but that is what the British Church appeared to try to make happen. The Council had envisaged a collaborative ministry which would involve a new partnership between consecrated sisters and the laity but this did not happen in the British Catholic Church in the late twentieth century. What actually happened was that many active consecrated sisters withdrew from their ministries and a large number of the laity left.

In regards to the male priesthood in Britain in the late twentieth century, there was a decline in the number of vocations but this was nowhere near as drastic as the decline in the numbers coming forward for the female consecrated life. This was because the male priesthood could not be forgotten as priests were needed to say Mass. However, what now tended to happen was that local priests continued to promote vocations to the priesthood but totally ignored vocations to the female consecrated life. Clericalism was on the rise. But it would not be fair to hold these priests totally accountable for this as the consecrated sisters themselves, as a result of a complete misunderstanding of the documents of the Council and a lack of drive, were failing to promote their own vocations believing that they might 'dominate things' and 'prevent lay people from taking up ministries'. These sisters were also unsure about their future roles as their ministries had been in teaching and most Catholic schools were now state schools. They seemed to find it difficult to adapt to new ministries unlike religious sisters in Catholic countries such as Italy. The result was that although there was a decline in vocations to the priesthood the ordained ministry did manage to hold up (just) but the female consecrated life was decimated and the laity did no better either. It is true that a significant minority of practicing Catholics took up the opportunities to be involved in lay ministries but a significant majority of lay people also left the church. Of course, there were many reasons for lay people leaving the church apart from the reasons discussed here. However, the withdrawal of the consecrated sisters from ministries post Vatican II was definitely, in the view of the writer, one of many factors that led to a decline in lay attendance at Mass in Britain in the late twentieth century. The Catholic Church had become an unbalanced one with no women in official full-time ministry.

The decline of the British Catholic Church and the female consecrated vocation in particular may perhaps now in the early twenty first century be beginning to flatten out although, as yet, it is still too early to tell. Since the time of the Second Vatican Council many new and restored forms of female consecrated life have come into being across the world and a new awareness of these is just beginning to develop in Britain but there still remains a very long way to go. These new forms of consecrated life do seem to have taken much better root in European countries other than Britain and Britain is very much lagging behind in promoting them. If Catholics in Britain do eventually develop a better awareness of the new and restored forms of female consecrated life this may ultimately lead towards a more collaborative ministry between consecrated women and laity in Britain but at the moment many lay people in Britain (particularly in Scotland and Wales) do still remain very much unaware of the many new and restored forms of female consecrated life that have taken off in other places in Europe. There has also sadly been some hostility from some bishops in the UK towards the new and restored forms of consecrated life. While some bishops in some dioceses have welcomed these new forms of consecrated life with enthusiasm and allowed them to grow, others have been very hostile towards them. They have refused to consecrate women as virgins in their diocese despite the fact that the vocation is officially approved by the church. The reason for this hostility has often been cited as the fact that these women live independently in their own homes and not in a convent. This smacks of misogynism as diocesan priests also live independently in homes allocated to them. The implication seems to be that priests can be trusted to live at home and keep their vows but consecrated women cannot.

In April 2015 it was widely reported in the British media that the number of women taking holy vows in the UK had trebled in the previous five years. Unfortunately, however, this report referred only to the number of women taking vows in convents. It did not include all the other women in the UK who were beginning to take vows in other forms of consecrated life which seem to have become much more commonplace in the rest of Europe than in Britain. In any case, despite this reporting, the number of women entering convents remained very low. The National Office for Catholic Vocations had stated that in 2009 there were 15 women who had taken holy vows and this had risen to 45 in 2015. There had also been some high-profile women who had left their jobs in order to test vocations to become consecrated sisters living and operating from convents. One of these was the BBC Northern Ireland reporter Martina Purdy who gave up her career in journalism in order to test her vocation. There had therefore been a small recovery in vocations to active consecrated sisterhood in the early twenty first century but it was not highly significant. What seems to be much more significant at this time are the 'new' or restored forms of consecrated life that are only now finally beginning to become better known in Britain. These forms of consecrated life are appealing to modern women because they do not involve living in a religious community and can be lived from an independent home base. There are currently around 230 consecrated virgins and widows in England but this number does not reflect the actual number of women who would like to be consecrated. A significant number of women in some dioceses in the UK have put themselves forward for consecration but the bishops in their diocese have refused to endorse or consider their vocations.

Chapter Seven

Female Consecrated Life In Britain Today

The female consecrated life in Britain today is, in regards to numbers, still in a state of crisis and there are some who believe that this way of life is 'finished' and will never rise again. It should be stated, however, that although this way of life is currently very much on the wane in Britain the current situation in no way equals that of the reformation when female consecrated life was completely obliterated on these shores. There have also been in recent years the signs of some increased interest in the female consecrated life although these remain small and, in regards to the new and restored vocations, have sadly been suppressed by some Catholic bishops on occasions.

The main problem in Britain that has led to such a drastic decline in the female consecrated life has been a severe decline in the religious congregations alongside either a lack of awareness of the new or restored forms of consecrated life or an unwillingness to embrace and promote the same. As the writer has previously stated Britain is different to the Catholic Countries in Europe because it has interpreted Vatican II in a more Protestant way. This has made the Catholic Church in Britain more clericalist than its counterparts in Europe and has resulted in a heavy emphasis been laid on the promotion of vocations to the male celibate priesthood and male married diaconate with vocations to the female consecrated life being almost completely ignored. Lay vocations are promoted in Britain but many of these (other than those taking part in educational settings) are very part time vocations which give women very little influence. In addition to this lay attendance at Mass in Britain is declining and so these vocations are doomed to struggle long term. The female consecrated life was always based on the ideal of a full-time ministry and, for the second time in the history of the Catholic Church in Britain, no full-time ministry for Catholic women is effectively promoted on these shores. The failure to promote the female consecrated life is noticeable in three Catholic groups:

Firstly, a certain number of the Catholic clergy do not promote the female consecrated life because they have noted the decline in religious congregations and therefore seem to have decided that the female consecrated life is 'finished' and not worth promoting. Some of these seem unaware of the other new and restored forms of female consecrated life. There are also some bishops who refuse to consecrate women to the new and restored forms of consecrated life.

Secondly the female consecrated life is not always promoted by the active religious congregations. Members of these congregations often do not even promote their own vocations and seem to have accepted their decline and declared that 'this is the time of the laity' although the number of lay people attending church is also declining.

Thirdly the female consecrated life is not always forcefully promoted by those small numbers of women in Britain who have embraced one of the new or restored forms of consecrated life. The writer has noticed that some of these women often seem to defer to the active religious (the congregations in decline) and almost seem to be afraid of offending them by promoting their own vocations. While it is always a good thing to respect the vocations of others, modern consecrated women do need to be aware that throughout history the forms of female consecrated life have continuously changed. The active religious congregations were dreamt up by Mary Ward in the early seventeenth century and were finally set up by others from the late eighteenth century onwards. This was a time when there were no welfare states and these congregations pioneered the creation of the same. It could be argued that they have now served their purpose and it is time for the new and restored forms of consecrated life to serve theirs. Most women in these forms of consecrated life live independently in the community. Some of these forms of consecrated life existed since New Testament times and have now been restored, while others are relatively new and emerged at a later stage. These forms of consecrated life have struggled to take root in Britain but have rooted much more successfully in other countries in Europe. The writer will now briefly examine some of them.

The Order of Consecrated Widows is one of the oldest female forms of religious life in church history since it existed in the early Church and is referred to in the New Testament (1 Timothy 5: 3-15). At that time, in order to be enrolled into this Order, a woman had to be at least 60 years of age, to have been married only once and to have lived a life of prayer and service to others following the death of her late husband. During this period there were also Orders of Virgins and Orders of Bishops and Deacons. (Rees 2015). However, the Order of Widows very quickly became well established in the early church and is mentioned by several of the early Church Fathers such as: St. Polycarp; St Hippolytus and St Jerome. These widows were mature women of faith who took part in the eucharist; prayed with psalms, hymns and meditations and were also known for their intercessory prayer. Generally speaking, these women lived in their own homes and Hylen (2018) states that in the Mediterranean world of the early centuries legal and social norms granted women property rights and substantial authority within their households and communities. While some widows may have been disadvantaged many others would have experienced only a slight drop in their economic or social status on being widowed or none at all. In the New Testament period and certainly up until at least the fifth century widows who were Roman citizens owned a substantial amount of property under Roman law and evidence would seem to suggest that Jewish widows were not that different from Roman widows and also owned their own houses. Therefore, these widows were generally ordinary homeowners who chose to use what they had and owned for the glory of God.

While it is known that there was an order of widows from New Testament times the origins of formalised chastity vows for widows in Britain (but particularly in England) are unknown. What is known is that vowing ceremonies for widows in England date back to the seventh century (Wood 2017) and these vowing ceremonies continued until the reformation. The widows who were to be consecrated were known as vowesses and they took a vow of chastity but did not take vows of poverty and obedience. However, before taking such vows these widows had to submit a formal request to their bishop and have their lives scrutinised to see if they were suitable for consecration. Rees (2015) states that the pontifical of the Anglo-Saxon archbishop of York, Egbert, includes a consecration of widows during Mass, and also a blessing of widows and their habit. The ceremony is later included in at least five 11th century pontificals. Generally during these ceremonies, the vowess was clothed in a mantle and veil and wore a ring which was blessed. Following their consecration vowesses were qualified by their vow to refer to themselves as brides of Christ. They were also free to own their own property and to live wherever they wanted. However, more importantly than that, they were free to select their own style of spirituality. They could decide whether to be a contemplative in action in the world or whether to be an enclosed solitary contemplative. Most of them decided to be contemplatives in action and carried out works of piety and charity in their community. They had a religious freedom which was to be completely destroyed by the reformation and from which Catholic consecrated women have yet to fully recover. After the reformation and right up until the early eighteenth century the church recognised only enclosed consecrated women, the active religious vocation of vowess having been completely suppressed. Eventually a new form of active consecrated life for women was approved but that involved living in a religious community. Women no longer had the right to live the consecrated life individually and their status within the

Catholic Church had been still further undermined. The fact that these vowesses were forgotten is extremely surprising bearing in mind that we have evidence that they were numerous. Ward (2017) states that Michael Sherbrook (c.1591) wrote that the number of consecrated widows, anchoresses and anchorites had far exceeded the number of secular priests prior to the reformation - 'all the said Religious Persons, which far passed the Number of the Secular Priests, there were many more, yea thousands, as Ancerers, both men and women; and widdows that had taken the mantle and Ring...' (Sherbrook 1591 cited by Ward 2017).

After the reformation it was to be 400 years before a movement began to restore the vocation of 'vowess' or consecrated widow. In the 1940's in France some war widows began to take vows. Later an acknowledgement of the spirituality of widows began under Pope Pius XII in 1957 when he addressed young French widows with children at home when attending the Congress of the International Union of Organisations concerning Family Life. His address was published in Osservatore Romano later that year. Pope Pius XII died in 1958. He was succeeded by Pope St John XXIII who called the Second Vatican Council. However little mention was made in regards to consecrated widows at this time. Later in 1967 and 1977 Pope St Paul VI addressed widows at Pentecost. By this time an increasing number of widowed women were once again beginning to consecrate themselves to God. In 1982, during the Hope and Life Pilgrimage to Lourdes, Pope St John Paul II made a special address to widows of faith. He later re-affirmed the consecration of widows in his encyclical Vita Consecrata which was published in 1996. Since then, the vocation of the consecrated widow has grown rapidly both in Italy and in France. It has also re-emerged in England where there are now around 30 widows consecrated. At the moment consecration is conferred by local diocesan bishops and is by local rite. However, at the time of writing the Prefect of the Congregation for the Institutes of Consecrated Life and Societies of Apostolic Life had advised the writer that practical proposals for a universal rite had been brought to the attention of the Holy Father for his consideration. Today consecrated widows take vows of poverty, chastity and obedience. They live fully in the world and report to their diocesan bishop to whom their vow of obedience applies. These widows often carry out work for the diocese but are not funded by the diocese. Consecrated widows are required to be financially independent and older widows may live off private or state pensions. However, they are expected to live a simple lifestyle in accordance with their vows of poverty. The younger widows often work full time in the secular world or in a more vocational position. Although today there are approximately 30 consecrated widows living in England there are currently no consecrated widows at all in Scotland although consecrations have been considered there but have never taken place. There appears to be some hesitation towards the vocation there which is not helped by the absence of a universal rite. This absence of a universal rite also leaves women wide open to abuse because it is possible for bishops to officially approve candidates and then change their minds and withdraw their approval at the last minute.

This does not happen with other vocations due to a clear process being defined in Canon Law.

The Order of Consecrated Virgins also dates back to New Testament times but it has had a different history to the Order of Consecrated Widows. This vocation is mentioned by St Paul in 1 Corinthians where he suggests a special role for unmarried women in the church. Chastity was praised as a religious virtue in the New Testament and it is believed that a consecration was imparted to virgin women by their bishops since the time of the Apostles. The first known formal rite of consecration is that of St Marcellina (353 AD). Initially consecrated virgins lived independently like consecrated widows. However, this did not continue for long probably because, unlike the consecrated widows, these virgins did not have the financial means to be self-funding in the world unless their parents supported them. During the medieval period women were still consecrated as virgins but by that time the consecration of virgins was maintained by nuns in monastic orders. This consecration was usually done concurrently with the profession of solemn vows. Thus, in medieval times consecrated virgins were living in monasteries. Their vocation was destroyed during the reformation as was the vocation of consecrated widow. During the early eighteenth century the enclosed religious life began to re-appear and the new form of active religious consecrated life (in line with that created by Mary Ward) was also developed. However, the rite of the consecrated virgin remained lost.

In the early twentieth century a return to the ancient practice of the consecration of virgins in the style of the early Church began to be supported by some forward-thinking French bishops. One bishop, François de Rovérié de Cabrières, the bishop of Montpelier, encouraged a young French woman called Anne Leflaive to seek consecration and she was consecrated on 6 January 1924 by the Bishop of Autun. After this event there was an increasing demand for these consecrations and the bishops sought clarification from the Congregation for Institutes of Consecrated Life as to whether they could proceed. However, the Congregation forbade this type of consecration stating that it had long fallen out of use. Leflaive, however, would not give up and in 1939 she founded the Secular Missionaries of Catholic Action which was an institute of celibate women living in the world. However, this institute was suppressed in 1946. After this Leflaive happened to form a friendship with Angelo Roncalli (the future Pope John XXIII) and he was receptive to her ideas. During the 1950's Leflaive began to visit Rome every year in order to lobby for the reinstatement of the rite of consecrated virgins. Leflaive also wrote a book about the vocation namely 'Espouse du Christ'. In 1952 Pope Pius XII issued 'Sponsa Christi'. This was a revival of the consecration of virgins but the Pope decreed that only enclosed nuns could receive the rite of consecration of virgin. However, in 1963 the Second Vatican council requested a revision of the rite of the consecration of virgins. The revised rite was approved by Pope St. Paul VI and published in 1970. The consecration could now be bestowed on women living in the world as well as women in monastic orders.

The first woman to be consecrated a virgin in England was Elizabeth Bailey. She was consecrated in 1972. Bailey was the first known consecrated virgin to live independently in Britain since around the fourth century. Bailey was consecrated at the age of 40 years. Initially Bailey trained as a midwife and worked as a missionary but after her consecration she worked as a Justice and Peace Worker for the Diocese of Plymouth. When asked why she had not become a nun Bailey stated, 'Give me one good reason why I should, originally consecrated people were pushed into convents because it wasn't possible for women to live on their own in the world. That's not true any longer.'

While this statement may actually have been true in regards to consecrated virgins it was not, of course, true of consecrated widows who had lived independent consecrated lives in their own homes right up until the reformation. Also in regards to consecrated virgins in the early church it is probably more likely that they went into convents because they did not have the means to support themselves independently in the world. Their parents would have wanted them to marry and a convent would have offered them an alternative from the married state.

Today there are approximately 200 consecrated virgins living in England. However, there are only two consecrated virgins living in Scotland where there continues to be a considerable amount of hesitancy towards the vocation which is very unfortunate as women there certainly feel called. These women are consecrated by their diocesan bishop who is their superior and to whom they are ultimately accountable. As has previously been stated not all bishops are willing to consecrate women as virgins and the writer finds this unjust and discriminatory. These vocations are legitimate vocations of the church which are enshrined in Canon Law and they should not be obstructed by bishops who feel that they do not want or like them. This is a suppression of the Holy Spirit which causes some women to have to move house in order to find a bishop who is sympathetic to their vocation. Women who do manage to be consecrated live a life of prayer and would be expected, like all consecrated religious, to pray the Divine Office at least in the morning, evening and night. But consecrated virgins are also women of action and could be termed 'contemplatives in action'. Many of them work and while a lot of them may work in a religious sphere, perhaps as a freelance religious affairs correspondent, a teacher of religious education or a spiritual director, others may work in the world in a completely secular job. On some occasions they might, perhaps, see no need to declare their consecrated status to secular people with whom they might work and might remain a hidden leaven in the world unless circumstances dictate otherwise.

A form of consecrated life that has, to date, always remained hidden in the world is the secular institute. A secular institute is an organisation of consecrated persons who profess the evangelical counsels of chastity, poverty and obedience but live independently in the world unlike members of a religious institute who live in a convent. Some secular institutes appear to have been founded in France under persecution at times when the French secular state was hostile to the active religious life. In France active religious sisters were driven underground due to state hostility and this led to groups of women meeting in secret and eventually, after a period of formation, being consecrated by their bishops in secret. These consecrated women saw themselves as a hidden leaven both serving others and secretly promoting the consecrated life within the world. The idea, however, of an active religious life lived by a group of people who met regularly but lived in their own houses began to spread throughout the world. Eventually restrictions were lifted in France in regards to the religious life but the secular institutes continued. These women continued with the new form of consecrated life that they had previously created under times of persecution and pressure. They lived in their own homes but met monthly in prayer and reflection perhaps for the whole weekend. They also participated in an annual retreat once a year which would last for a full week.

In 1947 secular institutes received formal recognition from Pope Pius XII in the document 'Provida Mater Ecclesia'. Today secular institutes are recognised either by a bishop (diocesan right) or by the Holy See. Most secular institutes are members of the World Conference of Secular Institutes. It is estimated that there are 60,000 members of secular institutes across the world. There are nine secular institutes in the UK and these belong to the National Institute of Secular Institutes (NCSI). However, once again within the UK, this form of consecrated life has not taken root in the way it has within other countries in Europe. After this form of consecrated life was approved by Pope Pius XII there was a surge of membership across Europe. However, within the UK, although secular institutes were created, they never achieved the numbers of consecrated members that occurred in for example France, Poland, Italy and also in other continents such as Africa. This may have been partially due to a reluctance of these women to fully promote their form of consecrated life in Britain, perhaps because they may have felt they were treading on the toes of some of the dying active religious orders. This lack of growth could also have been due to a reluctance of the Bishops of England and Wales and the Bishops of Scotland to take on board the new or restored forms of consecrated live that were being promoted by Rome. This is perhaps due to the fact that, as has previously stated, in Britain Vatican II has been interpreted in a very low church way.

Vatican II had promoted new lay ministries and in Britain the post Vatican II years were interpreted as the age of the laity with the active religious preparing to make their exit and the new and restored forms of consecrated life also being brushed aside. This was not the case in other European countries such as Italy where the active religious found other ministries such as working in the Vatican and the new secular institutes thrived. In Britain the new secular institutes were barely noticed. There was a small growth in numbers in the late twentieth century but by the twenty first century these institutes had already declined partly because some consecrated members had not grasped the opportunities open to them and sufficiently promoted their own way of life.

Today there remain a small number of members of secular institutes in Britain. Members of secular institutes here generally follow a seven-year formation path which in many ways parallels the formation of the active religious in convents. There is a short period of enquiry or postulancy which generally lasts about six months. After this the member becomes a novice and the novitiate can last up to two years. Once this period is completed the member will begin to take annual vows of poverty, chastity and obedience and these will be taken for at least five years and sometimes for longer until the member is either ready to make a final permanent commitment to the institute or decides to leave. Members can leave at any time during formation but once the final commitment has been made can only leave with the permission of their diocesan bishop (if the institute is diocesan) or the Holy See (if the institute is pontifical).

The life style of members of secular institutes is to be fully emerged in the world. Members live independently and support themselves financially. They are not however completely freelance and must meet certain obligations. Members might (according to the constitution of their institute) be expected to attend at least three residential weekends a year with other members and also an annual retreat of at least 7 days in length. Members would also be expected to attend the annual conference of the National Conference of Secular institutes. If their institute is part of a larger family (such as the Carmelite family) members might also be expected to attend a residential weekend with other members of that family such as religious sisters and friars. They might also be expected to attend Chapter meetings of their institute as and when these are arranged. This means that a considerable amount of a member's time might be spent away and the member would need to be able to combine this with whatever profession she might have. Generally speaking, a member might spend all her annual leave from work attending institute meetings and retreats. Never the less the secular institutes do provide a good setting for modern women who want to both pursue a career in the world and live the consecrated life and many members manage to hold down very demanding full-time jobs while meeting institute commitments. It is a great pity that this form of consecrated life has not been better promoted within the UK as it is possible the take up of this consecrated state would have been significantly increased if it had been.

Another restored form of consecrated life that is being practiced today is that of the consecrated hermit. This is quite a rare vocation which has its roots in the early Church. The first Christian hermits experienced a call to leave the world and seek God in solitude, austerity and prayer. Consecrated hermits are sometimes referred to as anchorites and there is some similarity between the lives of the current consecrated hermits and the pre-reformation anchoresses. However, the pre-reformation anchoresses, while living alone, tended to live attached to a Church in a cell and were often sought out by the laity for advice. Modern consecrated hermits publicly profess the three evangelical counsels and are consecrated by their diocesan bishops according to the Code of Canon Law 1983. They usually live alone in a remote location but might engage with the world for specific purposes. For example, Sr. Wendy Beckett produced a series of television documentaries on the history of art.

Having examined some of the new and restored forms of consecrated life above it remains to briefly examine the state of the enclosed religious life and the active religious life in Britain at these times. While there has been a decline in these forms of consecrated life the enclosed religious life does continue to hold its own and there are some forms of active religious life that have also managed to survive the current crisis.

Women living in the enclosed religious orders of the Catholic Church are the only women who, under canon law, are entitled to call themselves nuns. These enclosed religious orders have existed in Britain since around the time of St. Columba although they were of course suppressed at the time of the reformation and did not re-appear here until the early eighteenth century. Enclosed nuns are the only consecrated women to take solemn vows and they live separately from the world as members of a religious community in a house (usually a monastery) within enclosed grounds. Generally, an enclosed nun will not leave her enclosure unless she requires medical treatment. Some outsiders are, however, allowed to enter parts of the enclosure for a variety of reasons. The rules regarding outsiders entering the enclosure varies from community to community depending on their own particular constitutions. For example, in some communities lay people may just be allowed to enter the chapel for Mass and on these occasions will sit separately from the nuns. However other communities, such as the Tyburn nuns in Largs, run retreat houses. This community allows visitors into many parts of the enclosure as paying guests. The visitors will live with the nuns for a few days and join in with their worship albeit in a separate part of the chapel. The nuns will also cook meals for the visitors and sometimes even join with them for a meal. Nuns such as this run a self-funding community and the retreat centre provides them with a substantial amount of their overall income. There are also other religious communities who engage in this type of work and running a retreat centre is not unusual for enclosed nuns. These nuns do however remain enclosed and the people come to them rather than the other way round. Many of these communities, such as the Cistercian Bernardines at Hyning Monastery, also grow their own fruit and vegetables and make their own bread and cakes all of which are served to the guests. Anything they cannot produce is delivered to them so that they do not have to go out shopping in the community.

Enclosed nuns live a life of prayer which revolves around the Divine Office or Liturgy of the Hours. This is the Catholic Church's official set of prayers which marks the hours of each day and sanctifies the day with prayer. Enclosed nuns are expected to pray seven times a day with their communities but generally speaking they are also well able to combine this prayer with some kind of holistic business venture. Most enclosed religious communities are self-sufficient and manage to produce their own income through a variety of holistic occupations such as painting icons, making hosts for Masses, making religious cards and rosaries and opening their enclosures to paying guests. While this form of consecrated life is in no way thriving in Britain it is holding its own and managing to survive. This is perhaps because it could be argued that there will always be a small number of women who seek an enclosed and contemplative life.

Although the active religious sisters are generally in a state of chronic decline in modern day Britain there are a small number of active religious communities that have bucked the trend, managed to survive and have also created interest. Generally speaking, these are new religious communities that have modelled themselves in a different way to the declining religious communities. One such community is the Community of our Lady of Walsingham which is actually an Ecclesial Family of Consecrated Life rather than a religious congregation. This is a community of consecrated sisters, lay associates and priest associates. The community is based in Walsingham, England near the National Shrine of Our Lady. Its mission is described as, 'to hasten the coming of God's Kingdom by living in the joy of Mary's Fiat in the Divine Will. This we do by promoting a culture of vocation so that everyone can respond to God's love in their lives.' The sisters offer spiritual direction and vocational accompaniment as well as giving talks for young people in schools and hosting retreats and conferences.

Another religious community with a difference is the St. Andrews Community in Aberdeen. This community is actually comprised of a group of young individually consecrated virgins who state that they have come together in order to answer Christ's call for the New Evangelisation in our world today. These consecrated women live a life of prayer and adoration and their mission is with young people especially those who are disadvantaged. They are based near St Mary's

Cathedral in Aberdeen where they organise adoration of the Blessed Sacrament as well as running two youth groups and leading confirmation classes.

This chapter has summarised the current situation with regards to the Catholic female consecrated life in Britain today. It should be stated that there are also Anglican religious communities in existence in Britain but these have not been examined fully here as this book has been written with the purpose of promoting female vocations within the Catholic Church. In regards to the Catholic female consecrated life, while it can be seen that there are many promising shoots; in regards to overall growth this way of life is much depleted. However, this consecrated life is rescuable and the final conclusion will look at how the vocations to the female consecrated life can be grown and cultivated in Britain and also how the Church needs to look back to the future in order to increase the influence of women in its structures and communities.

Conclusion – Look Back to the Future

Having looked at the vocations and ministries of consecrated women from around 597 AD to date it can be seen that there is a very noticeable difference in the influence and status of the consecrated woman before and after the reformation. In the pre-reformation church, and in particular the pre-reformation church in England, there is evidence that consecrated women had a great more influence than they have ever achieved post-reformation. For example, in the Anglo-Saxon period, as has been noted in chapter one, both St Hilda and Aeffled voted at church synods. Both were abbesses of double monasteries and their positions gave them administrative and teaching authority over men who were priests. St Hilda taught theology to men who were priests and five of the men she taught later went on to become bishops. The double monasteries were eventually destroyed by the Danish raids but, despite this, women did not lose their influence in England. There were many singly vowed women who were either consecrated widows (vowesses) or anchoresses right through until reformation times. Although these women either attached themselves to a church or monastery (as in the case of anchoresses) or lived near to the same (as in the case of vowesses) they still led very independent lives and had considerable influence. Anchoresses were known for their spiritual direction and were sought out by royalty, eminent persons and priests for the same, while vowesses (vowed widowed women) were heavily involved in their local community in both guilds and fraternities. Some of them appeared to continue with projects that they had started with their late husbands' when they were married. For example, Margaret Browne had set up the Browne's Hospital in Lincolnshire with her husband before his death and she continued in her involvement of the same after his death. There is also of course the famous widow and visionary Richeldis who founded the shrine at Walsingham. It is very likely that she also was a vowess as these widows tended to be well born women who used their wealth for the furtherance of the mission of the Church.

The pre-reformation church, in England in particular, appears to have been a very different church in regards to consecrated women, to the post-reformation church. As Michael Sherbrook reminisced in 1591, there were more consecrated widows and anchoresses than there were secular priests. Unfortunately, however we only have rare glimpses of this fact. This is due to the fact that so much history and so many records were destroyed by Henry VIII when he decided to plunder and destroy the monasteries and we need to be aware that a lot of records that survived were the records that he wanted to survive and his intention was to wipe out the Catholic Church of his times from the face of England. For example the only reason why we have any knowledge of Julian of Norwich at all is because the enclosed Brigittine nuns, who were forced into exile at the time of the reformation, took Julian's book with them and continued to copy it. Similarly, additional information that we have about Julian of Norwich is found in 'The Book of Margery Kempe' which was the first autobiography to be written by an Englishwoman and a mystic and of course a pre-reformation one at that. Only one copy of this book survived and this came to light in 1934 when it was discovered by the Butler-Bowden family in one of their libraries. This family were a Catholic family but they stated it was very unlikely that the manuscript had been in their family throughout the centuries. They thought it may have been given to one of their ancestors at a later date as a gift from a recusant family who had kept it and hidden it throughout the reformation period. But the Book of Margery Kempe not only gives us glimpses of Julian of Norwich. It also gives us an example of a different pre-reformation England where religious married women were able to be independent and travel freely across the world in order to visit holy sites. Margery went on pilgrimages and travelled to the Holy Land, Assisi, Rome, Danzig, Norway and Santiago de Compostela. Of course, Margery may have been an exception amongst married religious woman. But how can we know that was the case? Most records of the pre-reformation church in England have been destroyed by Henry VIII. It is possible that prior to the reformation in England and elsewhere in Europe, England may have elevated the female consecrated and lay states more than other European countries. However, having said that, the desires for a new puritanism which would silence and strip such women of their independence are clearly seen in Margery's book. At that time women were allowed to preach but the Catholic Church in England was becoming more sexist and the Lollards were questioning Margery's right to do the same. All women in England were destined to lose their influence at the time of the reformation be they consecrated or lay.

At the time of the reformation in Britain the female consecrated life was completely eradicated but the male clergy survived. However, the male clergy that survived was not the clergy of the pre-reformation Church. In England Henry VIII wanted his own bishops and priests and he wished them to be subject to him rather than to Rome. He declared himself Supreme Head of the Church and Clergy in England and in 1534 passed the Treasons Act which made denying the Royal Supremacy an act which was punishable by death. As a result of this both Thomas More and John Fisher, who were later to become canonised Catholic saints, were executed. Henry VIII then went on to appoint his own bishops and clergy and also to take control over Church doctrine and ritual. In regards to consecrated women – these women hardly figured in the King's thoughts. Henry was minded to dissolve the monasteries because they were run by various religious orders that owned religious houses across the whole of Europe and thus were loyal to the Pope. He was also keen to seize their assets as his new regime was in financial difficulty. When these assets were seized it is known that some enclosed nuns who lived in some of the leading monasteries were pensioned off against their will. It was either that or they would lose their lives. It is also known that other enclosed nuns who had belonged to worldwide orders such as the Brigittine Order fled to Europe. However, there will have been still other enclosed nuns who were living in convents in Britain and who simply vanished from history. In the same way as all the anchoresses and vowesses in England simply vanished. There is no record of what happened to them. Pre-reformation they were numerous. Post reformation they simply disappeared.

As I have already demonstrated the Church in England took on an entirely different shape after the reformation to prior to the reformation. It became an all-male clerical church. Women no longer had any significance or importance. There were no full-time ministries available to women neither were there lay ministries. Women were wives and mothers. This did not change until the early eighteenth century when Catholic religious orders began to re-appear in the UK. At this time these members of religious orders were now fleeing from their own countries in Europe due to persecution there, their predecessors having originally fled from Britain due to religious persecution here. They began to thrive as active religious orders in Britain and eventually from 1841 onwards the Anglican community also began to establish its own religious orders.

While the female consecrated religious life was eventually 'resurrected' in Britain from the early eighteenth century this consecrated religious life was in no way the same as it had been prior to the reformation. Prior to the reformation there had been more forms of consecrated life than after it. Now the only options available to women were to live in a group either as enclosed women or as unenclosed women who could be active in the community. There was no room whatsoever anymore for any female independent consecrated life. Of course, many of the new active religious orders were made up of pioneering women who achieved great things. They built schools and hospitals and led social reform. But still women were diminished in post reformation England because if they wanted a full-time consecrated ministry in the Church the only option available to them was community religious life. Not all women are suited to or want a community form of life. Prior to the reformation there had been other options available to the more independent women.

The female active religious life which arrived here in the early eighteenth century has, having achieved many great things in the past, now fallen into decline. This is a result of many factors the main one being that the original ministry of these sisters had been to build hospitals for the poor and schools for uneducated girls and these functions were eventually taken over by the state. However, in other Catholic countries the loss of these ministries has not appeared to have had such a devastating impact on the active religious life as it has in Britain. This may be perhaps due to the fact that the clergy have been more supportive of their active religious there and other opportunities have been opened up for them. There has also been a less hostile environment for them in certain European countries as, since Henry VIII and his declaration of himself and those of royal line and descent as supreme heads of the Church in England, it could be argued that there has always been elements of anti-Catholicism in England. However, it is not only in England that the active religious life has declined. It has declined across the whole of the UK in the Four Nations of England, Wales, Northern Ireland and Scotland.

While the active religious life has declined in the UK there has also, at the same time, been a very poor take up of the various new and restored forms of consecrated life for women here. Again, this is in contrast to some other

European countries where these forms of consecrated life have become much more well-established. The main problem within the UK is not that these forms of consecrated life have been rejected by women who might seek consecration. It is rather that hardly any woman who might consider consecration has ever heard of them or even knows the slightest thing about them. It would be unfair to lay this ignorance entirely at the feet of the clergy as some members of these new or restored forms of consecrated life have themselves been either afraid or unwilling to promote their various vocations here. How many people have actually seen or picked up a leaflet in a church about a secular institute? How many women have seen advertisements about this way of life on line? The answer is very few or none and the same answer could also be given in regards to the life of a consecrated virgin or consecrated widow. The writer would argue that this is a great pity as it is possible that these new and/or restored forms of consecrated life could appeal to some committed Catholic women if they ever heard of them. Institutional religious life and religious congregations do not, in the main, appeal to the twenty first century woman. We live in different times now. Many women who might aspire to consecration prefer some kind of autonomy in the way they live their lives and, in addition to this, they might also wish to follow a modern career which would be in keeping with their vocation but not possible to follow while living in an institution. For example, one modern consecrated woman works as a director of a religious TV channel and travels all over the world with her work. Such a career would not be possible living in a convent. There are many other careers that women may aspire to follow in the modern world that would be in keeping with a consecrated vocation but could not be followed from the confines of a convent. These careers can give the secular consecrated woman a place right in the middle of the world from which she can be a leaven drawing in and attracting people to the Church and the Kingdom of God.

In addition to this it can also be argued that communal living in an institution that regards itself as spiritual but continues to mingle with the secular world from a point of distance can be unhealthy in modern society. Living in a religious congregation today places a consecrated woman in a position where she is neither in the world nor out of the world. She is somewhere suspended between the two and this is not always a good thing for a person's mental health. This was not the case when the religious congregations were founded as at that time consecrated women in congregations could be seen as very much part of a group that was not of the world but was trying to reform the world. Today this is not the case and sadly many of these women, while living in the world and not wearing a habit and mingling with lay others in church, still do not seem to be part of the world. However, as they do not wear the habit, they do not appear to be in some way separate from the world either. They appear to be slightly distanced from the world and to have a status which is slightly superior to the laity without any real reason for this. This can lead to communication barriers between them and the laity with a sense that the sister is 'holding back'. The consecrated women of religious congregations today are caught between expressing a fully secular consecrated spirituality or expressing a fully enclosed and distanced consecrated spirituality. The writer would argue that in our current times it is not possible to have a foot in both camps. A consecrated person will be a better witness being either fully in the world or fully out of it. Trying to be suspended somewhere between the two is not a position that the laity can identify with - hence the lack of vocations. And surely one of the objectives of being a consecrated person is to be able to identify with others in order to seek to draw them closer to God?

For these reasons it would seem that the new or restored forms of consecrated life better fit with the current world than the consecrated life offered by the religious congregations and it is time that these were now fully promoted. By coming to this conclusion, the writer is in no way seeking to undermine the religious congregations of today as their illustrious history can be clearly seen in all that has been written about them in this book. The writer also recognises that there are a small number of religious congregations that have managed to maintain some kind of influence and ministry in Britain. However, what can also clearly be seen is that most of the religious congregations no longer fill the needs of the time or offer women of today a form of consecrated life that they can live in the current world. It is therefore time for all consecrated women of the restored or new rites to promote their vocations with vigour and it is time for the bishops and clergy in Britain to be more sympathetic to these women and to assist them to do the same. These women can play a vital part in evangelising and promoting the faith because they live and work in the world side by side with the laity. They are on the same level as lay people and they understand secularity and are able to help others to live a spiritual life in a secular world.

Finally, there have been many debates since Vatican II as to whether women should be ordained to the priesthood. However, within the Catholic Church this is a schismatic issue with some scholars arguing that there is no historical evidence that women were ever priests. Our society now has an idea that every role a man occupies a woman should also be able to occupy otherwise the two are not equal. But surely in the early church men and women were equal without holding the same roles? The issue here is more about women having an equal voice in the church rather than consecrating the eucharist and this can be achieved by being true to history. Women were never priests but they did vote at church synods. Surely the way to give women an equal voice in the church in a way that is not schismatic would be to create female lay cardinals?

Lay cardinals have previously existed in the church and a lay cardinal was a cardinal in the College of Cardinals who was a lay person and had never been ordained as a deacon, priest or bishop. Lay cardinals seem to have existed from the sixteenth to the early twentieth century and all were men. It could be argued, however, that the status of the early abbesses who had the power to vote at church synods was not that different to the status of these lay cardinals.
In 1917 the new Code of Canon Law dispensed with lay cardinals and it was decreed that from then on only those who were priests or bishops could be chosen as cardinals. However, because there exists a precedent for lay cardinals,

there is actually no reason why they cannot be reintroduced and in 1968 Pope Paul VI proposed appointing the French Catholic Philosopher Jacques Maritain as a lay cardinal. Maritain, however, refused the honour. The role of lay cardinal could be seriously considered by the Vatican as a way to give both consecrated and lay women a stronger voice in the Church while at the same time being true to history. The problem with the modern Catholic Church, particularly in Britain, is the lack of official full-time ministries for women which has led in recent years to an increasingly patriarchal leadership. The writer would argue that the Catholic Church was never so patriarchal in the past.

Citations

Anglo Saxon England (Stenton)
History Today (Mitchell)
Edith the Fair Visionary of Walsingham (Flint)
Consecrated Widows (Rees)
The Shrine of Our Lady of Walsingham (Dickinson)
Women Religious (Thompson)
In Search of Julian of Norwich (Upjohn)
Julian of Norwich: The Teaching of a 14th Century English
Mystic (Molinari)
A History of England (Trevelyan)
English Social History (Trevelyan)
Medieval English Nunneries (Power)
Works of Geoffrey Chaucer (Pollard)
The Convents of Great Britain (Steele)
Vowesses in the Province of Canterbury (Wood)
A History of English Christianity 1920 – 1985 (Hastings)
Women in the New Testament World (Hylen)
The Falle of Religiouse Howses, Colleges, Chantreys, Hospitals
(Sherbrook 1591 cited by Ward 2017)

Works Cited

Stenton Frank *Anglo Saxon England.* Oxford at the Clarendon
Press (1943).
Mitchell Barbara *History Today Volume 45* (Issue 10 October
1995)

Flint Bill *Edith the Fair Visionary of Walsingham* (2015)
Gracewing

Rees Elizabeth *Consecrated Widows* Pastoral Review (2018)

Dickinson J.C. *The Shrine of Our Lady of Walsingham*
Cambridge at the University Press (1956)

Thompson Sally *Women Religious* Oxford University Press
(1991)

Upjohn Sheila *In search of Julian of Norwich* Darton, Longman
and Todd Ltd (1989)

Molinari Paul *Julian of Norwich: The Teaching of a 14th
Century English Mystic* London: Longmans Green (1958)

Pollard Alfred *The Works of Geoffrey Chaucer* Macmillan
London 1907

Trevelyan G M *A History of England* London: Longmans Green
& Co (1926)

Trevelyan G M *English Social History* London: Longmans
Green & Co (1942)

Power Eileen: *Medieval English Nunneries* Cambridge
University Press (2010)

Steele Francesca: *The Convents of Great Britain 1902*
Reprinted by Creative Media Partners LLC (2015)

Wood Laura Mary *Vowesses in the Province of Canterbury*
Royal Holloway University of London (2017)

Hastings Adrian: *A History of English Christianity 1920 – 1985*
Collins (1986)

Hylen Susan: *Women in the New Testament World* Oxford
University Press (2018)

Sherbrook Michael – *The Falle of Religiouse Howses, Colleges,
Chantreys, Hospitals* (1591) Cited by Ward 2017

Bibliography

Bede: *Ecclesiastical History of the English People (673-735)* Penguin Classics (Revised edition 1990)

Herrin Judith: *The Formation of Christendom* Fontana Press (1987)

Farmer David Hugh: *The Oxford Dictionary of Saints* Oxford University Press; (Third edition 1992)

Gallyon Margaret: *The Early Church in Wessex and Mercia.* Terence Dalton Ltd (1980)

Godfrey John: The Church in Anglo Saxon England. Cambridge University Press (2009)

"Women in Viking Society." ukessays.com. 11 2018. UKEssays. 03 2021

Von Nolcken Christine: "The Wrath of the Norsemen: The Vikings and their Memory," online article for Fathom Archive, 2001,

Hilda of Whitby (accessed June 2018): http://en.wikipedia.org/wiki/Hilda_of_Whitby

How Did Christianity come to Britain? United Christian Broadcasters Rev Robert Pickles http://www.ucb.co.uk/content/roots-map

Glastonbury Thorn - Wikipedia The Free Encyclopedia (accessed 5 August 2017) http://en.wikipedia.org/wiki/Glastonbury_Thorn

Rees Elizabeth. *Consecrated Widows* Pastoral Review (2018)

Ridyard Susan: *The Royal Saints of Anglo Saxon England:* Cambridge University Press (1988)

https://en.wikipedia.org/wiki/Nathalie_Becquart

The Guardians of the Shrine of Our Lady of Walsingham: Walsingham England's Nazareth (1969)

Bond H.A: *The Walsingham Story through 900 years* Greenhoe Press (Revised edition 1964)

https://en.wikipedia.org/wiki/Richeldis_de_Faverches

https://en.wikipedia.org/wiki/Our_Lady_of_Walsingham

Rees Elizabeth: *Consecrated Widows* Pastoral Review (2018)

Burton Janet: *Monastic and Religious Orders in Britain 1000-1300* Cambridge University Press (1994)

Anonymous: *The Life of Christina of Markyate* Oxford University Press (Oxford World Classics Paperback 2008)

Kempe Marjory: *The Book of Margery Kempe* Penguin Classics (1994)

The Oxford Illustrated History of Christianity Oxford University Press (1990)

Fleming David: *The Fire and the Cloud: An Anthology of Catholic Spirituality* Geoffrey Chapman (1978)

Baker Denise: *The Showings of Julian of Norwich* W.W. Norton & Co (2005)

Clark Katherine *The Profession of Widowhood: Widows, Pastoral Care and Medieval Models of Holiness* The Catholic University of America Press (2018)

https://en.wikipedia.org/wiki/Ancrene_Wisse

https://en.wikipedia.org/wiki/Julian_of_Norwich

https://en.wikipedia.org/wiki/Christina_of_Markyate

Edwards David: *Christian England* Collins (1981)

Matthew David: *Catholicism in England* Longmans Green & Co (1936)

The Catholic Encyclopaedia

Knowles David: *The Religious Orders in England* Cambridge University Press (1950)

Wood Laura Mary: *Vowesses in the Province of Canterbury 1450 -1540.* Royal Holloway University of London (2017)

https://en.wikipedia.org/wiki/Mary Ward (nun)
https://en.wikipedia.org/wiki/**Edward VI** of England
https://en.wikipedia.org/wiki/**Syon** Monastery
Chaucer – Tales of Caunterbury (1400) Reprinted Penguin Classics
Anson P F: *Religious Orders and Congregations of Great Britain and Ireland* Stanbrook Abbey Worcester (1949)
Beck George A: *The English Catholics (1850 – 1950)* Burns, Oates London (1950)
Anson P F: *The Call of the Cloister* S.P.C.K. London (1955)
Essays by Various Writers: *Catholic Emancipation 1829 – 1929* Longmans Green & Co London (1929)
Jedin H: *History of the Church Volume VII.* Crossroad Publishing Company New York (1981)
The Conciliar and Post Conciliar Documents of Vatican II
http://www.ukvocation.org/
https://en.wikipedia.org/wiki/Second Vatican Council
https://en.wikipedia.org/wiki/Charles Davis (theologian)
The Telegraph 23 December 2007
The Guardian 24 April 2015,'why I answered the call to convent life.'
Lumen Gentium (1964)
https://en.wikipedia.org/wiki/Sacred Heart
https://en.wikipedia.org/wiki/Humanae vitae
Vita Consecrata (1996)
Consecrated Virgin Wikipedia
https://en.wikipedia.org/wiki/Consecrated virgin
Community of Our Lady of Walsingham
https://www.walsinghamcommunity.org/
Callum P H: *Vowesses and Female Lay Piety in the Province of York (1300 – 1540)* Northern History 32. (1996).

http://www.ukvocation.org/
https://en.wikipedia.org/wiki/Lay_cardinal